Brigitte et Gilles Delluc
Alain Roussot
Julia Roussot-Larroque

Discovering
Périgord
Prehistory

Alain Roussot, director

Brigitte et Gilles Delluc, Doctors in prehistory, UMR 6569 of the CNRS
Alain Roussot, Honorary Curator-in-Chief of Heritage
Julia Roussot-Larroque, prehistorian

ÉDITIONS SUD OUEST

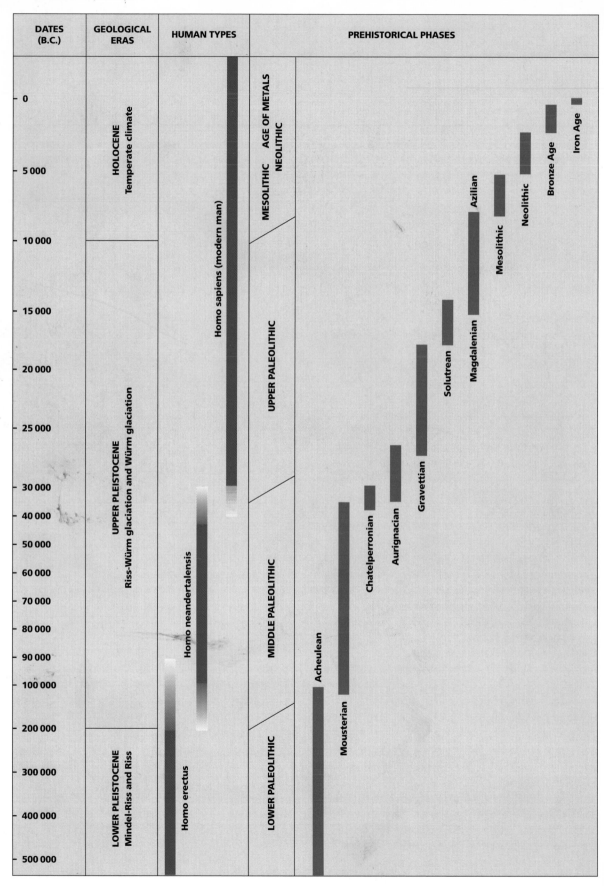

Chronological table of prehistoric and protohistoric times (see too p. 66).

Frost from a cold winter whitens the area at the base of cliff in Les Eyzies, whereas the heat of the sun reveal a recently plowed field. This same image evokes the notion of the glacial climate of the reindeer age, as it gradually give way to the milder times of agriculture.

Two or three million years: a brief summary

Everywhere humans lived, they left behind a few bones, tools and weapons made of stone, bone, or metal, a few grams of charcoal, small pebbles, and virtually invisible grains of plant pollen. However, these odds and ends would be of little importance to us, if we were unable to breathe life into them.

Therein lies the work of the prehistorian (or protohistorian for work in periods closer to recorded history).

In understanding human history, one needs to be able to distinguish Christopher Columbus from Karl Marx, or Gutenberg from Napoleon. Understanding prehistory and protohistory requires a great deal of patience as one progresses step by step on the elusive paths of knowledge. Rosny's *Quest for Fire* mistakenly lumped together ancient humans, early hominids, Neandertals, and our immediate ancestors, Cro-Magnons.

But these are successive periods, and we invite you to explore them with us in the Périgord region. It is here that, since earliest times, prehistoric and protohistoric humans have come to live.

The dawn of time

The great age of our planet is truly staggering. Four billion years ago, the earth was formed. Life, a tiny blue algae, appeared 2 billion years later. Dinosaurs walked the earth 200 million years ago, and the first humans emerged only 2.5 million years ago in Africa. Only in the past 450,000 years have humans colonized the Périgord region of France. The Cro-Magnon rock-shelter was occupied only 35,000 years ago, and Lascaux was decorated just 17,000 years ago. In short, human prehistory is very recent. Now let us try to present it in an ordered perspective.

Geological periods are divided into eras (primary, secondary, tertiary and quaternary eras). One of the main features of the quaternary era is the presence of Man. Three major periods succeeded each other during this era – the Paleolithic (Lower, Middle and Upper) or Carved Stone Age, the Neolithic or Polished Stone Age and the metal ages. Each of these major ages is divided into several periods, usually reflecting the appearance of the implements

The Neandertal man.
This human skull, unearthed at la Ferrassie, did not belong to our direct ancestor, but rather a Neandertal. He lived in Les Eyzies area about 40,000 years ago.

The first modern human.
This skull belonged to the most famous of our direct ancestors the people of Cro-Magnon. This was one of five individuals discovered in 1868 under the small rock-shelter of Cro-Magnon near Les Eyzies train station. Nicknamed the 'old man', he was probably no more than 50 years which was already quite old for this time period. This 'race', or to put it more accurately, this type of human did not emerge first in the Les Eyzies region. Its predecessors were found in the Mousterian of the Near East. Thus, in the words of Yves Coppens, the people of Cro-Magnon were thus migrant workers!

made of stone or bone by Man. It was this industry which characterised the cultural aspect of the civilisation. The name of each period is derived from the name of a major site on which extensive traces of the period have been found. The site is described as "eponymous" (Aurignac and the Aurignacian Period, La Gravette and the Gravettian Period etc.).

The chronology established by Carbon 14 dating is indicated either as B.P. ("Before Present") i.e. before "the present" fixed, by convention, as 1950 A.D. or as "calendar" dates (B.C., "Before Christ") using other methods. The latter dates are often several centuries older because it was noticed that Carbon 14 "years" were often shorter than actual annual periods.

For the Paleolithic Age, the dates are usually given as "B.P." since current methods do not allow for their calibration.

Four successive human types

Three million years ago, just prior to the emergence of the first humans, several small creatures appeared. They had poorly developed brains, walked erect, and subsisted by hunting. These were the Australopithecines of South and East Africa. One among them, Lucy, has become a big celebrity. Even her name was borrowed from a popular Beatles's song.

The first human was *Homo habilis* – a maker of stone tools. *Habilis*, who was also African and lived by hunting small, easily captured, prey (e.g. lizards, small birds) and gathering, and made pebblestone tools. These were used as much for cutting as they were for scraping, hammering, and digging. These "handy" humans were short (less than 1.5 meters high), their brains were rather small (650 cm^3, or half that of ours), but the morphology of their bones indicates that they walked erect.

Their teeth also resemble our own more than they do those of an ape. They had no forehead, and possessed a heavy brow ridge that hung over their eyes; their jaws were robust and without a chin. *Habilis*' language is believed to have been very rudimentary. The color of their skin is, of course, unknown. They appeared in East and South Africa 2.5 million years ago and persisted for approximately one million years.

Homo erectus made their debut almost 2 million years ago in Africa, Asia, and Europe. The oldest French skeleton is of this type was from Arago cave near Tautavel in the Eastern Pyrenees. *Erectus* discovered the use of fire around 400,000 years ago. They lived in wind breaks made of branches, as in the case of Terra Amata, near the port of Nice. Their tool assemblage consisted of hardly more than a simple but ingenious tool type: the biface (or hand axe). It consisted of a rounded flint nodule, more or less flat and oval, with a cutting surface on all the edges. The biface was the all-purpose tool.

Homo erectus were no larger than their predecessors; their skulls retained more or less the same primitive characteristics, but their brains were larger (1000 to 1200 cm^3, or a third of ours). The endocasts, taken of the insides of the skull, show that they possessed an articulate language. They were also hunters and even hunted mammoths (in the marshlands of Spain). In the hunt, they concentrated on archaic elephants, deer, wild boar, and small aurochs (wild oxen). This long period was marked by alternating cold and temperate climates. Some of the last *Homo erectus* occupied La Micoque rock-shelter in Les Eyzies. These were the first "inhabitants of the Périgord", but skeletons have yet to be uncovered at this site.

100,000 years ago, new, somewhat rustic and robust humans appeared. They were slightly taller than their predecessors (1.6 meter) and had very large brains. They developed occipitals, sloping foreheads, proeminent brows and lacked chins. These were the Neandertals whose stone tool industry is known as Mousterian. Neandertals were no brutes. They made superior tools such as impressive bifaces, but also scrapers, points, and blades. They collected fossils and minerals, and the presence of ocher and manganese crayons indicates that they developed an appreciation for colors. They buried their dead in caves like La Chapelle aux Saints in Corrèze.

The last and most recent in this lineage were the Cro-Magnons who were every bit as human as ourselves. Indeed, we are all Cro-Magnons or *Homo sapiens*. We emerged 30,000 to 35,000 years ago and were no more or less attractive or intelligent than we are today. Naturally, Cro-Magnons did not have the same culture as we do. They manufactured tools from blades extracted from a large flint core (end scrapers, drills, burins, and points) and from animal bone and deer antlers (increasingly diverse forms of hunting weapons). They learned to sew, and made ornaments and a medley of other objects. They also quite suddenly began to depict by drawing and sculpting small figurines. Cro-Magnons appeared during the Upper Paleolithic, Neandertals were of the Middle Paleolithic, and the most ancient humans existed during the Lower Paleolithic.

Warm and cold spells

Over the course of these millions of years, the climate was not always the same. Four long periods of cold called glaciations were interrupted by periods of warming known as interglacials. The two last glaciations bear the name Riss (500,000 to 125,000 B.C.) and Würm (115,000

Bernifal cave (Meyrals).
The Dordogne boasts thousands of caves, several dozen of them decorated during the Paleolithic period.

to 10,000 B.C.) which were derived from two tributaries of the Danube where the glaciers in the basin of this river have been studied.

During these glaciations, the climate was clearly more rigorous than today (5°C cooler on average), and resembled present-day Scandinavia with a typically periglacial fauna (mammoths, reindeer, musk ox, woolly rhinoceroses, arctic foxes, and ptarmigans) and flora (a retreat of the forest and particularly deciduous plants, with only lichen, moss, a few clusters of willows, and dwarf birches during the extremely cold periods). During these cold periods, the climate varied with latitude and altitude, proximity to the sea or mountains, from year to year, and from century to century. When the thermometer rose slightly, a marshland of alders, birches, and pines emerged in what constituted a taiga. A few degrees warmer produced a climate similar to ours and not unlike the interstadial of Lascaux 17,000 years ago. A change in the fauna and flora followed accordingly. Neandertals and Cro-Magnons lived during the Würm glaciation. However, it would be a mistake to imagine them living on some sort of icebank occupied by polar bears or suffering through blizzards and the long polar nights. They were not Inuits. The study of the animal bones (large herbivores, as well as small mammals and birds), plant pollens, and wood and mineral residues permits us to reconstruct the climate.

Countless caves

There are numerous caves in limestone areas. The rock is naturally fissured, with vertical cracks (diaclases) or horizontal cracks (stratification joints) that are widened by underground streams which gouge out galleries, some wide, some narrow. Later, these ducts are partially filled

In Les Eyzies, about 20,000 to 25,000 years ago, during a very cold phase (Abri Pataud Museum).

with clay soil and by concretions of calcite (stalactites, stalagmites, flows etc.).

Man made settlements at the mouths of caves, or used them as the last resting-place of the deceased. Cro-Magnon Man, especially from the Lascaux period (17,000 years ago), went deep into the galleries and passages to decorate the rock walls, in the trembling light of tallow lamps. These decorated caves are places of worship, underground sanctuaries. Some of the decorated caves are fairly close to the surface, e.g. the cave in Saint-Cirq. Most of them, however, consist of deep cavities which are sometimes difficult to access, among them Font-de-Gaume, Lascaux, les Combarelles, Bernifal, Villars in Dordogne, Pech-Merle and Cougnac in Lot, Niaux in Ariège and Altamira in Spain.

A few of them are vast, running over a distance of several miles, such as the cave in Rouffignac which visitors can now see from a small electric train.

Places to live

From the earliest points in human prehistory, humans have built living structures – huts with frames made from branches (or even from the tusks of mammoths in the great plains of Russia which were covered by skins, and carpeted with furs). These structures were erected either in the open or beneath the overhang of a cliff that formed a rock-shelter or in the opening of a cave. *Homo erectus* at Terra Amata built a hut and even erected a small wall to protect themselves from the wind.

The Cro-Magnons, like us, sometimes even paved the floors of their huts as was the case in the lower Isle valley. However, these "cave dwellers" never actually lived inside these dark, humid, and quickly smoke-filled cavities. They often buried their dead in caves or ventured (sometimes quite far) into their depths to paint and engrave images on the walls.

The humans of the Paleolithic Périgord hunted, fished, and gathered their food. They lived off the land without agriculture and husbandry. They led a life of semi-nomadic hunters, settling briefly in one area and then later moving on in search of game and reindeer in particular, which regularly travel long distances during their migration.

The successors to the men of the Paleolithic Age saw the huge herds of reindeer heading back northwards as the climate became more clement. During the Neolithic and metal Ages, Man settled in rock-shelters, at the mouths of caves or in the open air. They buried their dead beneath dolmens then in burial grottoes. Since farming, stock-breeding, metalworking and ceramics aroused a degree of envy, they made weapons to defend themselves again other men, and built the first fortifications. By convention, Julius Caesar's conquest of Gaul and the end of the siege of Alésia in 52 B.C. mark the end of the prehistoric period and the beginning of the great History of France.

The great range of animals

Not unlike the flora, the fauna also vary with the climate. During very cold periods, musk ox, mammoths, wooly rhinoceroses, reindeer, wolves, and smaller animals (weasels, hares, white foxes, ptarmagins, and snowy owls) thrive.

When the climate warms, a covered forest becomes home to mousses, bison, although reindeer, mammoths and wooly rhinoceroses persist. In the open clearings, large herds of reindeer, horses, and droves of wild oxen (aurochs) abound especially during seasonal migrations. Ibexes and chamois flourish on the high plateau, when they are not taking refuge in the high mountains. Felines hunt primarily at night, and cave bears retire to their caves to hibernate, drop their cubs, or die. (Caves bears were of the Mousterian period and were later succeeded by the brown bear in Cro-Magnon times).

What happened when the temperature rose a little more? Temperate forests appeared (with oak, hazel, Norway pine, junipers, and sometimes even walnut trees) intermixed with prairies populated by horses, aurochs, red deer, hinds, roe-deer, boars, and species of small animals that are still known today.

A historic excursion.
When they arrived in Les Eyzies in August 1863, Lartet and Christy descended upon this small cavity that was once called grotte Richard. A small fragment of an archeological layer from this, exhibited in Paris in 1862, and inspired them to make the trip. Located in a cliff overlooking the Beune valley in Les Eyzies, this cave was occupied briefly in the Solutrean but predominantly in the Late Magdalenian.

A fossilized living floor. Hardened by the infiltrations of calcium enriched water, the archaeological level from grotte Richard can be cut into blocks or plates. Lartet and Christy sent samples of these to several museums including the Musée du Périgord. This 'breccia' contains worked flint, cobblestones, animal bones – especially reindeer – that humans hunted and ate, and occasionally, small pieces of engraved stones or bones (Musée du Périgord).

Dates and people

Prehistory proceeded by trial and error for nearly two centuries before becoming recognized as a true science. Today, it is taught in our universities. Several dates will illustrate the principal steps of this long path of progress from the early 19th century, a time when the great antiquity of humankind had not yet been recognized.

1810. A professor and occasional letter-press printer, François Jouannet, explored Ecornebœuf, a site which overlooks the modern city of Périgueux formed on the ancient city of Vésone. There, he collected flint arrow-points flaked and polished axes that he attributed to the Gauls.

1815-1816. Jouannet explored Pech de l'Azé cave near Sarlat, and Combe Grenal cave near Domme. In both cases, worked flint was found in association with animal bones. Jouannet wrote that "What we have seen bears the characteristics of the greatest antiquity".

1834. Based on collections, Badegoule cave near Lardin, the Jouannet suggested that a stone age existed that predated that of polished stones and of bronze, and yet Jouannet still attributed this stone age to the Gauls.

1847-1860. The publication of *Celtic and Antediluvian antiquities* by Jacques Boucher de Perthes officially marked the birth of prehistory thanks to geological, paleontological and archaeological observations made in the Abbeville region (in the valley of Somme).

1863-1864. Edouard Lartet, a magistrate in the Department of Gers, and Englishman Henry Christy, Lartet's friend, patron, and manufacturer arrived in Les Eyzies in August 1863. For several months, they walked along the banks of the Vézère valley and explored some of the most prestigious sites: the grotte des Eyzies, the vallon of Gorge d'Enfer where one rock-shelter bears Lartet's name, Laugerie-Basse, Laugerie-Haute, La Madeleine, Le Moustier, and others. This period marked the beginning of an intensive period of excavations in the region.

1868. Several human skeletons dating to the Aurignacian period were uncovered in association with flint tools, beneath a small rock-shelter, near the train station in Les Eyzies. In 1874, Armand Quatrefage and Ernest-Théodore Hamy used these skeletons to define a new fossil race – Cro-Magnon.

1872. A skeleton was discovered near Laugerie-Basse which was also associated with worked flint, bones, and

A classic photograph. This 1897 photograph of the engraved and painted "hut" was taken for E. Rivière in La Mouthe cave – the first decorated cave to be discovered in the Périgord region in 1895. In order to insure that it not be published without his consent, Rivière printed it in blue making it impossible to reproduce at the time (see p. 42).

worked reindeer antler. The same year, the French Association for the Advancement of Science visited Les Eyzies for its first conference. This date marked the start of archaeological tourism in the region. In 1883, The Joanne Guide already had already begun describing the principal sites of interest in the region.

1874. This year saw the creation of the Société historique et archéologique du Périgord which to this day publishes numerous works on the region's prehistory.

1888. Maurice Féaux and Michel Hardy exhumed a Magdalenian skeleton in front of the small Raymondien cave near Chancelade.

1895. Engravings and paintings were discovered in La Mouthe cave in Les Eyzies. They were found in a corridor which was uncovered far end of the cave's entrance where Emile Rivière had been excavating since 1894. It was the first decorated cave discovery in the Périgord, the third in all of Europe, after Altamira in Spain and Chabot cave in the Gard.

During the second half of the 19th century, several archaeologists excavated known sites and discovered still others. Gradually, a more exact chronology of prehistoric periods was developed (by E. Lartet, Gabriel de Mortillet, and Edouard Piette). However the research methodologies were often too hurried and unorganized. A significant number of sites were destroyed forever. It was not until the 20th century that properly conducted excavations were undertaken, notably by Denis Peyrony.

1900. Chance discovery of a small full-round sculpture cal-

led the "Venus of Sireuil" in the rut of a wagon track.

1901. September 8. Louis Capitan, Henri Breuil, and D. Peyrony explored the Grotte de Combarelles where they discovered wall engravings. On September 12, Peyrony observed paintings and engravings in the cave of Font-de-Gaume. These two finds, in addition to the discoveries made at La Mouthe cave, contributed to the official recognition of the antiquity of cave art, which until then was questioned by a few archaeologists.

1908. A Swiss antiquary, Otto Hauser, who ransacked sites in the Périgord, found a Neandertal skeleton in Le Moustier and sold it immediately to the Berlin Museum.

1909. At La Ferrassie, Peyrony, who had excavated there since 1902, uncovered one of the first of many Mousterian human burials. Others were found between 1909 and 1921.

1909. The excavation at the abri du Cap Blanc in Marquay yielded an animal frieze sculptured on the rock-shelter's back walls. It was the first discovery of parietal sculptures.

1910-1913. Peyrony undertook a state funded excavation of La Madeleine where three phases of the Upper Magdalenian are clearly defined.

1911-1912. Bas-relief representations of human beings were revealed in the abri du Laussel near Cap Blanc but from an earlier period. In 1912, a sculpted fish was discovered on the ceiling of a rock-shelter in the Gorge d'Enfer in Les Eyzies.

1913. December 31. A law was passed concerning historic monuments, which guaranteed the protection of all present and future prehistoric sites. The same year, at Peyrony's suggestion, the government bought the ruins of the Château des Eyzies to convert it to a museum. The first exhibition opened in 1918, and the museum was officially inaugurated in 1923.

1921-1935. Peyrony excavated at Laugerie-Haute. This important site allowed the development of an exact chronology for several phases in the Upper Paleolithic and complemented the Ferrassie chronology.

1931 and 1933. Discovery of a cache of 27 bronze axes near Thonac. These finds were later protected by the State in 1943.

1934. Maurice Vidal found a Mesolithic skeleton at Roc du Barbeau near Le Moustier.

1937. Paul-Emile Jude exhumed an Azilian skeleton in the grotte de Rochereil near Lisle in the Dronne valley.

1940. Discovery of Lascaux cave which was authenticated immediately by the Abbé Breuil. Major alterations allowed Lascaux to be opened to the public by 1948.

1941. September 27. A law was enacted which influenced the regulation of archaeological excavations. Passed by the Vichy government and validated in 1945, it specified that all future excavations were subject to government authorization.

1950. Prehistory was introduced to the academic curriculum and later granted its own degree program in the Faculty of Science at the University of Bordeaux. The program was initially led by Georges Malvesin-Fabre (1950-1956), followed by François Bordes (1956-81), François Prat (1981-1989), Henri Laville (1989) and others after.

1953-1954. Hallam L. Movius excavated a major Aurignacian and Gravettian site in Pataud.

1953-1965. F. Bordes excavated Combe-Grenal, a large Acheulean and Mousterian site.

1956. Led by Charles Plassard, Louis-René Nougier and Romain Robert discovered prehistoric drawings in the already well-known cave of Rouffignac.

1957-1959. F. Bordes and Philip Smith excavated Laugerie-Haute.

1959. Henri Delporte unearthed a female figurine in the excavations at abri Facteur in Tursac.

1963. Lascaux cave was closed to the public when certain algal growth and calcite deposit threatened the preservation of the paintings.

1967. F. Bordes reopened the excavation of Pech de l'Azé which he had initiated in 1948.

1968-1978. H. Delporte undertook the re-excavation and re-analysis of the large shelter of La Ferrassie.

1969-1981. Jean-Philippe Rigaud excavated Grotte Vaufrey near Domme.

A few years before the Great War.

In 1908, a Bordeaux medical doctor and scholar, G. Lalanne, directed large scale excavations beneath the abri du Laussel, six kilometers up the Beune valley from Les Eyzies. This photo of the "dig site", taken in 1911-12, speaks for itself. However other archaeologists of the time, like Denis Peyrony, conducted more careful and meticulous excavations.

This is a sample of the dates that have marked the history of research in the Périgord. We have not been able to cite all of them here, nor have we included the more recent work which is either in progress or as yet unpublished. To this list, we might also add numerous discoveries of cave art, some of them quite recent, often made with the help of resourceful Périgord speleologists.

Tour 1
From 450,000 to 35,000 years ago
The Lower and Middle Paleolithic

A very old living site.

Over 100,000 years ago, Acheulean peoples returned on several occasions to live at the base of a small rocky escarpment near the Manaurie stream, not far from the Vézère River. There are almost ten meters of archaeological deposits, the uppermost being a final Acheulean with elongated bifaces, with concave sides and finely retouched points. These are known as Micoquian bifaces.

It is difficult to specify when the first humans occupied the Périgord. The discovery of primitive-looking tools in very old alluvial deposits has occurred here and there by chance, especially in the Isle valley. Some of these may have been abandoned by *Homo erectus* during the first two Quaternary glaciations (Günz and Mindel).

It was not until the third glaciation – called Riss – that true living sites are found in this region at Pech de l'Aze, La Micoque, and at Grotte Vaufrey where lower strata date to 450,000 years ago. These layers contain industries characterized by bifaces – stone tools worked on both faces – and tools made using retouched flakes such as points, scrapers, notched tools, backed knives, etc. These industries bear the name Acheulean (from Saint-Acheul on the outskirts of Amiens in the Somme valley where they were first defined in 1872).

Several varieties of Acheulean industries are defined on the basis of distinctive shapes of bifaces, the presence or proportions of certain tools, and the knapping technique used. Acheulean variants include Southern Acheulean, Clactonian (as defined by H. Breuil at Clacton-on-Sea in England), which is equivalent to the Tayacian described by Peyrony at La Micoque, Micoquian (which is a facies of Final Acheulean also found at La Micoque), and others.

A significant discovery dates to this Acheulean period – the controlled use of fire and the ability to light and maintain fires. This is confirmed by the numerous, organized, and structured fire pits that were discovered by François Bordes at Pech de l'Azé.

In the Périgord, no human remains have been recovered from this period, and the possibility of finding any is minimal since funerary rites and organized burials were not yet practiced at least not in living sites. However, in the Eastern Pyrenees, the Caune de l'Arago has yielded several human bones including a large part of the face of a skull, and scattered remains mixed in with worked stone tools and animal bones.

Had the Acheuleans already developed a sense of aesthetics? Many bifaces share a uniformity in size and regularity in form which suggests that the artisan went beyond the need to create efficient tools.

In the Riss glaciation, a new industry appeared which differed from the Acheulean and bore closer resemblance to Mousterian industries found later with *Homo neandertalensis* in the Early Würm glaciation. Thus, at least in its beginnings, the Mousterian emerged as a technique rather than as an actual culture. This technique is found 200,000 years ago at Grotte Vaufrey, La Micoque, and is at times interstratified with the Acheulean.

The Mousterian appeared during the Riss glaciation and developed and diversified in the Early Würm between 115,000 and 35,000 years ago. It was discovered in 1863-64 by Lartet and Christy at Le Moustier. In 1869, G. de Mortillet proposed to name comparable industries "Moustier Types" and in 1872 called the corresponding period the "Mousterian" (formerly written Moustierian).

Le Moustier, the eponymous site, was excavated more thoroughly in the early 20th century by Peyrony, and its industries were studied more closely around 1950 by François Bordes and Maurice Bourgon. The Mousterian forms an industrial complex composed of several distinct facies distinguished by their technology and typology. Bordes defined five major groups. Cordiform or triangular Bifaces were still present in certain cases (Mousterian of Acheulean tradition). There was a diversity of tools made from flakes composed of more than sixty, well-defined, retouched types of which points and above all scrapers were characteristic.

A means of knapping known as Levallois technique was developed in the Acheulean. This procedure consisted of shaping a block of raw material (a core), such that a flake of predetermined shape could be detached, then possibly adding retouch to make a tool. The presence of this knapping technique characterizes certain Mousterian assemblage types.

The Mousterians occupied a wide area of the Périgord and often lived in open air sites, on plateaux, in valleys, and also beneath rock-shelters or in shallow caves.

Neandertals lived in this period. They often buried their dead in organized and sometimes complex burials within living sites. Pits were dug, surrounded by stones, or covered with flagstones. Such funerary practices continued and diversified in the Upper Paleolithic.

About 35,000 B.C., the last Neandertals were replaced by *Homo sapiens*. For a short period, called the Chatelperronian, the two groups may have co-existed, but perhaps no living in the same groups.

An all-purpose tool.
The biface (or hand axe) is a block of flint, cobblestone, or a large flake with retouch on two faces, more or less tapered on one end and more or less rounded on the other. The first bifaces go back to very ancient times in Africa. In Europe, they are typical of the Lower Paleolithic and the Mousterian, and different forms characterized different periods. Variable in size, they may have served to break bones, cut branches, or possibly to scrape hides.

La Micoque

This famous site which opens to the southwest, is located on the right bank of the Manaurie rivulet, 500 meters above its confluence with the Vézère, just upriver from Laugerie-Haute. It is not a rock-shelter, but rather an open-air site at the base of a small limestone cliff about fifteen meters above a modern stream and a bank of river cobbles.

Discovered in 1895 by E. Rivière, the site was excavated indiscriminately by several archaeologists, especially by the antiquarian Otto Hauser from 1906 to 1914. It was nevertheless he who created the term "Micoquian" in 1916, to describe an industry peculiar to the site. This term was used again by Breuil in 1932, following excellent exca-

Ghostly timbering.
In Combe Grenal, during a dig carried out by F. Bordes, differences in sediment revealed the shape of a sharpened peg, originally made of wood, in a Mousterian layer, and a cast was made.

A complex excavation.
One hundred meters from the cave site for Pech I and Pech II, lies a large Mousterian talus site called Pech de l'Aze IV, which is situated against the cliff wall. It was discovered by F. Bordes (centre) who defined over twenty archaeological strata which in turn were further subdivided into several levels. At a such a site, it is difficult to excavate the same layer across the site's entire surface. Therefore the excavation was carried out in meter squares, and the data were recorded and regrouped stratum by stratum in maps and profiles.

vations conducted by Peyrony from 1929 to 1932, and after the site had been acquired by the state. In 1956, Bordes conducted a test excavation at La Micoque. In 1969, H. Laville and Jean-Philippe Rigaud completed a detailed stratigraphic study, and in 1983 a multi-disciplinary team of researchers has renewed an in-depth study of the site.

The stratigraphic sequence at La Micoque is important to understanding the region's Lower and Middle Paleolithic, since the six successive occupations there correspond to the Riss and Early Würm glaciations.

The oldest Rissian industries, or even pre-Rissian industries, are in general composed of flakes which Peyrony attributed to Tayacian and Breuil associated with the Clactonian (levels 1 and 2). According to F. Bordes, levels 3 and 4, previously thought to be Tayacian, contain two Mousterian facies: One Quina (or Charentian), and the other Levallois. These two levels are contemporaneous with the Riss glaciation and thus are much earlier than the Early Würm glaciation which was formerly believed to correspond to the start of the Mousterian.

The top layer of the site contains Micoquian industries (Final Acheulean) characterized by elongated bifaces with wide bases, fine points, and slightly concave edges.

This Micoquian tradition, at its eponymous site, is believed to date to the Early Würm glaciation.

Le Pech de l'Aze

From Sarlat to Carsac, a road and an obsolete railroad track follow the small Font de Farge valley in which a now defunct stream once flowed into the Enea River, a tributary of the Dordogne. Four prehistoric sites are found at the foot of a limestone outcrop which crowns Pech de l'Azé hill (which means Donkey hill in the local vernacular). Pech I and II are located at the two extremities of a 60 meter long cave which passes through a limestone outcrop. The first entrance is of historic importance because it was probably the first prehistoric site to be explored in the Périgord (by Jouannet in 1815). In the 1818 issue of the *Calendrier de La Dordogne*, he described with astonishment the bones that had accumulated in the cave together with small fragments of black flint. Jouannet writes "How far back in time did this barbaric workmanship and unique deposits originate? We know not. If we speak of this cave in a work on the Gauls, it is only because all we have seen bears the characteristics of the greatest antiquity".

Later, a number of archaeologists visited the cave including Lartet and Christy in 1863. More recent excavations were undertaken by Peyrony in 1908, by René Vaufrey in 1929, by François Bordes and M. Bourgon in 1948 and 1951. The latter two discovered the second entrance to the cave or Pech II. From this moment forward, Bordes dedicated several years to the excavation of Pech de l'Azé, explored a small nearby cave (Pech III), and discovered a vast collapsed rock-shelter, Pech IV, 100 meters downstream.

The entire complex made a major contribution to a deeper understanding of the Lower and Middle Paleolithic, since the lower layers of the oldest strata were dated to the Mindel-Riss interglaciation and contain an Acheulean industry. The strata correspond to the Riss and Early Würm glaciations. During the same span of time, the climates, fauna, and flora varied with the climatic fluctuations from warm periods to cold or extreme cold periods in which reindeer were already quite abundant.

In Pech II, the incontestable presence of hearths demonstrates that humans controlled fire as early as the Acheulean. These were dug in the ground, sometimes surrounded by fire-reddened stones, and contained burned soils and blash ash.

Several iron oxide and magnesium oxide chunks with scraping marks, were recovered from Mousterian strata. Some were even shaped into "crayon-like" implements. In one of the strata, Peyrony and Capitan also discovered an isolated crushed skull of a four year old child.

An eponymous site: le Moustier.
Le Moustier is on the right bank of the Vézère at its confluence with the Vimont valley. Village houses rise in tiers on the rocky steps of the limestone outcrops at the angle formed by the two valleys. Two superposed rock-shelters have been excavated since 1863, and the industries found there have aided in classifying the Mousterian.

Le Moustier

The small village of Le Moustier is perched on the point of a rocky promontory formed by the intersection of the Vézère River as it flows beneath La Roque Saint-Christophe and the Vimont valley which descends from Plazac to the north. This promontory is accentuated by a series of terraces, the top one of which contains a small, shallow cavity – le trou du Bréchou.

Within the village itself, the classic rock-shelter was explored in 1863-1864 by Lartet and Christy. It was this upper rock-shelter that later gave its name to the Mousterian period and industry. Ten meters lower, a second rock-shelter was excavated in the early 20th century, first by the antiquity dealer – Otto Hauser in 1907, and then later by Peyrony after the French government purchased the site in 1910.

Unfortunately for French archaeology, in August 1908, Hauser uncovered a human Neandertal skeleton which he named *Homo mousteriensis hauseri*. The remains were sold, at a high price, to the Berlin Museum where the skull was repeatedly – at least four times – and poorly reconstituted. It was believed that this skull was pulverized during World War II bombings, but the skull reappeared several years later in a laboratory in Iena in the former East Germany. It might well be studied in more depth one day, but no reliable information is available on the burial itself.

Today, we are more familiar with the human occupation of the higher rock-shelter and especially the lower rock-shelter, thanks to the excavations of Maurice Bourlon and Peyrony in 1905 and of Peyrony in 1910, and due to research on stone tool industries initiated by Bordes including the stratigraphic and sedimentological observations made by Laville and Rigaud in 1969.

The Mousterian occupation occurred in the two initial stages of the Würm glaciation and was followed by brief occupations in the Chatelperronian and Aurignacian at a time when the two rock-shelters were nearly completely filled. In each occupation, the habitat also extended beyond the shelter's rocky overhang.

Peyrony, and especially Bordes, defined several types of stone tool industries characterized by tool types and their proportions in the overall tool assemblage. These facies do not seem to correspond to different populations but rather to varying activities.

A distinctive tool.
The bifacial tool, point and scraper are the three "main indicative fossils" of the Mousterian Period but more than sixty other shapes have been described. In addition to flint, hyaline quartz (rock crystal) was sometimes worked, as here in Laussel. At the bottom right is a Levallois nucleus showing a detached flake of a shape predefined by the preparatory cutting of the stone (Musée d'Aquitaine).

COUPE
DU
GISEMENT

DEBLAIS
AURIGNACIEN
I

PÉRIGORDIEN
I

MOUSTÉRIEN
TYPIQUE

SABLE
FLUVIATILE

MOUSTÉRIEN
DE
TRADITION
ACHEULÉENNE

A control section for the Mousterian.
Despite the numerous successive excavations at Le Moustier, one section of the rock-shelter's lower filling was preserved. Thus, we can see here the superposition of several Mousterian levels, below two Upper Paleolithic levels (Aurignacian and then Chatelperronian). In other words, occupations which stretched from about 70,000-50,000 to 32,000 years ago. A wall has been built in front of the section, and a cast evokes a part of the stratification.

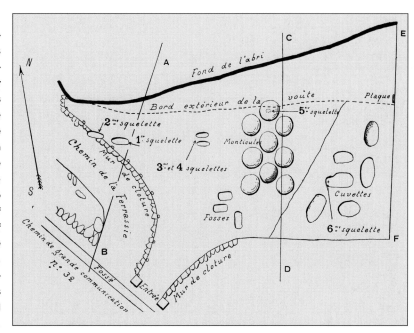

La Ferrassie

This site is somewhat off the beaten path, midway between Savignac-de-Miremont and Le Bugue, in a small valley which joins the Vézère at Le Bugue. Facing south, the large rock-shelter is at the intersection of the valley and a small vallon. The site sits at the side of a road whose very construction led to its discovery in the late 19th century. Very soon thereafter, amateur archaeologists made their way to La Ferrassie. These included Denis Peyrony, a young grade school teacher in Les Eyzies, who arrived at the site in 1896. For thirty-three years, Denis Peyrony made La Ferrassie his "home-base research site" in collaboration with L. Capitan who bought the site in 1923 and later sold it to the state.

The rock-shelter's overhang was invisible at the start of the research, because it was masked by a broad (40 meters long and 20 meters wide,) talus. Little by little, Peyrony's excavations were able to reach the rock-shelter's fillings from successive occupations, as well as the large fallen blocks resulting from the regular collapse of the rock-shelter's overhang. By the end of the excavation, Peyrony had succeeded in excavating one hundred square meters of the site and had partially revealed the rear wall of the rock-shelter. Peyrony left behind two, six-meter, high stratigraphic profiles – one longitudinal and the other transversal.

Much later, between 1968 and 1973, H. Delporte renewed research at La Ferrassie. Starting from the control sections which he cleaned up, Delporte excavated only a small section of the archaeological filling but worked meticulously to clarify the details of the site's stratigraphy.

As we shall see later, La Ferrassie is a major site in the region's prehistory, especially in the earliest stages of the Upper Paleolithic, the Aurignacian and Gravettian. It was in fact at La Ferrassie and later at Laugerie-Haute and La Madeleine that Peyrony documented the successive human occupations of the Périgord. H. Breuil used these data on several occasions to establish his subdivisions of the Upper Paleolithic cultural chronology on a much larger scale.

La Ferrassie was the scene of significant discoveries for the Mousterian. From 1909 to 1921, Peyrony brought to light several human burials and various features associated with them. These remarkable finds made under controlled excavation conditions, made up for Hauser's disgraceful period in Le Moustier in 1908.

By the end of Peyrony's excavation, which was published in 1934, he was able to map all of the burials and associated features such as pits, depressions, and mounds, which are spread out over the entire explored surface.

On the left, two pits, each facing east-west, contained a 40-45 year old man and a 25-35 year old woman respectively. In another pit to the right, a 10-12 year old child was buried, and a fourth pit nearby held the remains of either a foetus brought to term or a 15 day old newborn child. In front of the rock-shelter, three empty pits and eight mounds were found. One mound yielded seve-

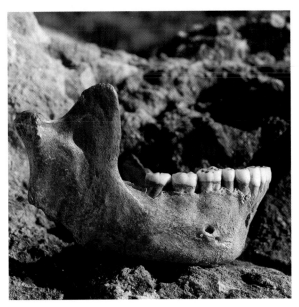

A Solid Mandible.
Several skeletal remains were preserved from this Neandertal burial, including bones in the upper body, the vertebral column, and the sternum. However, no cranial material survived except this impressive robust mandible whose teeth were barely worn (Musée du Périgord).

ral bones of a seven month old child which was placed in a depression. Finally, one of the large depressions to the right contained the remains of an approximately three year old child whose skull was buried in the pit 1.25 meters from the body. The head was separated from the body at its interment or shortly before. In addition, this burial was covered by a large limestone gravestone bearing small pecked depressions. Delporte found a second child of approximately two years near the rock-shelter's wall near the mounds.

This is definite evidence of a funerary rite which was exceptionally complex for its time. It is also exceptional for the presence of young individuals whose ages range from newborn up to early adolescence. The remains of human adults contributed to a detailed study of neandertal characteristics. (The male is one of the best examples from this group). The remains of the younger individuals of various ages have contributed to an understanding of Neandertal growth and development. For example, it was observed that the maturation of the skeleton occurred at a faster rate than it does today, which accounts for the primitive characteristics.

Le Régourdou

The circumstances of the discovery of the site and of Régourdou's Mousterian burial are, to say the least, picturesque. Some five hundred meters from Lascaux, on the edge of the plateau overlooking the Vézère valley and the city of Montignac, Roger Constant, a resident of the small hamlet of Régourdou, aided the Abbé André Glory in his study of Lascaux and even lived there on occasion. Convinced that an alternate entrance existed to Lascaux than the one currently recognized – one that he believed to be the original prehistoric entrance to Lascaux –, Constant excavated in front of his small farm. While he did not find an alternate entrance to Lascaux, he did discover a Mousterian site and a human burial in September 1957.

The Régourdou site is a vast rock-shelter site whose overhang collapsed after its archaeological filling. Following a chance discovery in 1957, the excavation was entrusted to two prehistorians, Eugène Bonifay and Bernard Vandermeersch, who worked from 1961 to 1965. Once the rubble from the overhang was cleared, they encountered several occupation levels containing Quina type Mousterian which was characterized by scrapers with flaked retouch and dated back to the beginning of the Würm glaciation.

The human burial was in a shallow pit, carefully capped by a flagstone and surrounded by a small wall of rubble. The body lay on its left side, the head facing North, with the knees bent under the chin and the hands brought towards the head. A fairly large sized limestone flagstone covered the trunk, while stone blocks and sand covered the rest of the burial. A fire was subsequently lit on this small burial mound, but it is unknown whether it is truly related to the interment.

A significant number of skeletal remains, including the sternum, were preserved. Unfortunately, the skull was not preserved but a well preserved and robust mandible was recovered with all its teeth intact and barely worn. Adjacent to this human burial, there were also stone structures, paving, and lined pits or receptacles containing the bones and skulls of brown bears. In one deep and 1.5 meter-long pit, marked by small walls of stone and covered by a heavy flagstone, were the remains of a skull and bones of a single bear.

This complex ritual is very puzzling. The relationship between humans and bears (a bear cult?) had already been suggested based on earlier discoveries in Swiss and Italian caves, although their ritual or religious interpretations were sharply criticized by A. Leroi-Gourhan. Needless to say, Bonifay and Vandermeersch's observations were disconcerting.

From 35,000 to 20,000 years ago. The Aurignacian and Gravettian (or the Upper Perigordian)

Modern humans appeared some 35,000 years ago. The first 25,000 years of their existence corresponded to the end of the last glaciation called the Würm. This time period, the Upper Paleolithic, began with the Würm III – the coldest phase of this glaciation.

The oldest modern type humans, the first *Homo sapiens*, are commonly known as the Cro-Magnons. This name was derived from a rock-shelter situated in the village of Les Eyzies where the first fossil remains of these humans were found in 1868.

The last Mousterians

The transition from the Middle Paleolithic was embodied in the Chatelperronian civilization (35,000 to 30,000 B.C.), which is known from Chatelperron cave in Allier.

It is clearly defined at La Ferrassie above a series of Mousterian levels and beneath an Aurignacian sequence. The Chatelperronian is also present at the Abri du Moustier. It is a period in which the climate became progressively cooler

This "Mousterian disguised as Upper Paleolithic", as Leroi-Gourhan would say, consisted of a combination of Mousterian type tools, a Mousterian-Levallois knapping technique, and Upper Paleolithic forms (burins and end scrapers). It is characterized by a tool with a curved back called the Chatelperron knife. At this time, the first true bone tools appeared which were essentially awls and a few sharpened bone antler fragments. The Chatelperronian layers at Arcy-sur-Cure in Yonne are famous for yielding the oldest bone pendants, the oldest bone with paired incisions, as well as Neandertal teeth. The discovery of a skeleton of a Neandertal male in the Chatelperronian at Saint-Césaire in Charente-Maritime reinforced once again the notion of the transitional role this civilization played.

The first Cro-Magnons

The Aurignacian (about 32,000 to 20,000 B.C.) is the first of the Cro-Magnon culture. It was widespread in Europe (Spain, France, Central Europe, and Italy) and extended as far as the Near East. The excavation of several large sites in the Périgord –La Ferrassie, Castanet, and Pataud – served as basic references for all prehistorians.

The Aurignacians were subjected to an environment that alternated from harsh and dry climate with steppe-like grasslands to phases of increased humidity during

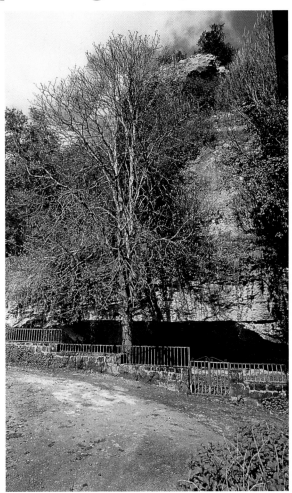

The Cro-Magnon's rock-shelter.

This rock-shelter is located between Les Eyzies and Tayac. It was discovered in 1868, five years after the first prehistoric study was undertaken by Lartet and Christy in the Périgord. Creating a railroad track bed, workers unearthed the first known burial of modern-type human fossils. Carved out at the base of the cliff which borders the Vézère River's west bank, approximately 250 meters upriver from Abri Pataud, the site is today hidden behind the Cro-Magnon hotel, although signs and arrows direct the visitor. This small overhang whose ceiling collapsed at the time of excavation, was first a campsite for Aurignacians (25,000 to 30,000 years ago) before serving as a burial place. The human remains (at least three men, one woman, and a newborn child) were discovered near the top of the archaeological deposits which nearly completely filled the rock-shelter.

La Ferrassie's large rock-shelter (Savignac-de-Miremont).
Above the Mousterian strata, a succession of Aurignacian and Gravettian occupations yielded works of prehistoric art – notably engraved, sculpted, or painted stone blocks.

A stone engraved with vulvar images from La Ferrassie.
This large limestone block (56 x 40 cm) from the Aurignacian III bears two deeply engraved images of vulva surrounded by depressions. Other dotted or finely incised lines may be traces of complementary images (Musée des Eyzies).

A painted abri broken in fragments (Abri Blanchard, Sergeac).
The Aurignacians at the Abri Blanchard also painted the ceiling of their rock-shelter, which collapsed due to frost during the coldest period of the Würm glaciation, thus shattering the decoration. On a large wall fragment, one can still read the black lines against a red background, which depict the limbs and ballooned stomach of an animal that probably represents a horse. The rest was destroyed. From 1910 to 1911, abri Blanchard was studied by Louis Didon and his trusty excavator, Marcel Castanet (Musée du Périgord).

The Aurignacian Tool Kit. In addition to the classic end-scrapers, burins, and perforators made on blades by all Upper Paleolithic hominids, the Aurignacians made a range of flint tools on thick blades, and also spear-points and other implements of bones and reindeer antlers.

which tree growth increased. Throughout this period, reindeer were the most common animals, along with horses and red deer (during less cold conditions) or mammoths and woolly rhinoceroses (when the climate became cooler).

Aurignacians developed implements which lasted throughout the Upper Paleolithic (end-scrapers, burins, perforators). But each period had its specialties. In the Aurignacian, end-scrapers were very abundant (more than 50% of the tools), blades were thick and sometimes narrow, and readily made using scalar retouch, which produced a large number of small flakes. Based on the composition of the tool kit and the shape of the bone points, an Early Aurignacian (I at La Ferrassie) is associated with split-based bone points, Middle Aurignacian (II at La Ferrassie) with more or less thick lozenge-shaped bone points, and a later Aurignacian (III and IV at La Ferrassie) with thicker bone points.

It was at this time that figurative drawing was born. It was an extraordinary Cro-Magnon invention which consisted of reproducing in two dimensions what existed in nature in three dimensions. In Southern Germany (bade Wutemberg), Aurignacians invented the full-round sculpture. They sculpted small statues representing animals and human beings. Here, in the Périgord, along the Vézère, and within a 15km radius of Les Eyzies, half a dozen Aurignacian camps beneath rock-shelters, yielded engraved or sculpted limestone blocks which were intermixed with artifacts of everyday life. The drawings usually consisted of female sexual images, rudimentary animals which were often incomplete, and puzzling geometric signs. In addition, since the beginning, humans decorated the overhangs or walls of their shelters with images made with strokes of paint, engraved lines, and applications of color. However, the extreme cold of the period, led to the deterioration of the walls exposed to the elements and as a result nothing is found in place today (Musée national de Préhistoire, Les Eyzies). Our knowledge of the decorations stems from the fallen, identifiable,

Sculpted phallus (Abri Blanchard near Sergeac).
The Vallon des Roches in Sergeac seems to have been a favorite place in the early Upper Paleolithic. Located on the right bank, Abri Blanchard was occupied on several occasions by Aurignacians (I and II). These occupants left behind about 15 decorated stone blocks. These are precious examples of the first representations of humanity and include female and male sexual signs (vulvas and phalluses) and animals deeply incised in limestone blocks. At the very base of the site, near a 30,000 year old hearth, was the oldest figurative art object to be discovered in France: a phallus made from the bony base of a bovid's horn (Musée des Antiquités nationales).

The Belcayre kid (Thonac).
The Grotte de Renne of Belcayre is located less than a kilometer from the Vallon des Roches on the opposite (right) bank of the Vézère River, at the base of a row of collapsed cliffs. It was not excavated until 1923 or 1924, when Frank Delage found two Aurignacian levels. The most outstanding discovery was of a single block, decorated with the pecked image of an ibex. Shortly thereafter, the site was disturbed and the work was halted (Musée des Eyzies).

fragments that were recovered from the archaeological strata in sites like Blanchard, Castanet, La Ferrassie, Le Poisson, and Abri Pataud. In Périgord, very few caves have decorations that date to this period. These caves are small with heavily eroded walls upon which an organized system of images can be seen. In Bernous, near Bourdeilles, three rudementary animals are aligned in a frieze, and in La Croze-à-Gontran at Les Eyzies, panels of animals are separated by geometric signs.

The discovery of the amazing Chauvet Cave in Ardèche, in which the decoration has been so well preserved, showed that, originally, men also decorated large underground sanctuaries with very elaborate designs. Howe-

Engraved lines as fine as hair (Abri Labattut, Sergeac).
The Gravettians at the Abri Labattut left the most diverse
examples of their artistic skills. One extraordinary, small (10
cm.), fine-grained, limestone pebble bears the finely engraved
and carefully detailed image of a horse with a hatched mane,
an eye, a beard, and hoofs. However, despite the abundance of
detail, the style is still archaic with a ballooned stomach, short
neck, long head, and lack of perspective in the limbs. The nature
of the surface probably had a considerable influence on the
quality of the image's details (Musée de l'Homme).

ver, for the moment at least, they are very rare and nothing like this has yet been discovered in Périgord. The superb engravings in the Pair-non-Pair Cave in Gironde, not far from Le Bec d'Ambès, probably date from these distant days. The animal decoration is very well structured around a shaft of light but is in poor condition because of the type of rock.

... And then came the Gravettians

The Gravettian (25,000 to 17,000 B.C) is the second of the largest civilization of the Upper Paleolithic. It extends across Europe from Spain to Russia, all the way to the Don. But the largest number of known sites is concentrated in the Périgord. It is possibly for this reason that prehistorian Peyrony, founder of the Musée national de Préhistoire in Les Eyzies, designated this culture the Perigordian. He believed he could subdivide the Perigordian into six periods (I to VI). He later abandoned Perigordian I, II, and III, but continued to use the terms Perigordian IV, V, and VI to designate the unique stages of the Gravettian civilization. An additional stage was added to mark the terminal stage of the Gravettian – the Perigordian VII. At the time of its discovery at Laugerie-Haute, the Perigordian VII was called the Proto-Magdalenian by Peyrony. However, the name is deceiving since this industry, which is older than the Solutrean, does not belong to the Magdalenian sequence.

Several famous sites in Périgord were occupied during the long periods of the Gravettian, among them the eponymous site La Gravette, in the Couze valley, and Laugerie-Haute in Les Eyzies. However, it was not until the excavation of the Abri Pataud between 1958 and 1964, that a complete stratigraphic sequence with all the Gravettian

stages was revealed. As a rule, the term Gravettian is used to describe the civilization as a whole and especially its oldest phase. In the Périgord, the subdivisions are specified by using the terms Perigordian IV, V, VI, and VII.

The climate at this time was very cold. It was interrupted by several temperate episodes (such as the Tursac interstadial), during which tree growth resumed in the more open clearings.

The flint tool assemblage became more diversified and specialized. Burins dominated (over 30%), followed by a large number of truncated burins, and relatively fewer end-scrapers. La Gravette points are present in every phase in variable proportions. Small arrowpoints are found the Perigordian IV, small Noailles burins, Font-Robert points, and some truncated elements in the Perigordian V, and long truncated blades in the Perigordian VI. In the Perigordian VII, the stone tools are composed of up to 40% burins and approximately 30% backed bladelets. Bone tools are always present but are not very characteristic (awls, pierced batons, and bone points) and ornaments are abundant (pierced shell, teeth, bone).

In Périgord, cave art was still essentially limited to the walls of rock-shelters and associated with art on stone blocks. During this period, two very remarkable caves

The Gravettian Tool Kit.

In addition to the classic end-scrapers and burins found throughout the Upper Paleolithic, the Gravettian industry is characterized, in all strata, by the presence of Gravette points: straight backed blades, sometimes veritable darts, which were hafted onto the ends of very efficient hunting weapons. Other stone tools allow for further subdivisions to be made – the small Bayac arrowpoints ("flechettes") in the Périgordian IV, and Font-Robert points, truncated blades, and Noaille burins in the Périgordian V. The bone material is composed of awls and oblong bone points with or without a single bevel.

A Gravettian hand.

This hand imprint on the roof of Le Poisson rock-shelter in Les Eyzies is outlined in pale black and is the oldest known negative hand, along with the one found in the Labattut Shelter in Sergeac on a block of stone which has fallen into one of the levels of the same period.

were decorated: Gargas in the Pyrenees, and Cosquer near Marseille. The classic techniques of painting (as in Labattut) and engraving (from Oreille d'Enfer, Pataud, and Laugerie-Haute) were used, and sculptures (such as at Laussel and Le Poisson) became of considerable importance. Animal silouhettes were still rudimentary and in simple profile, but the species were identifiable. Sexual representations were present but appeared less frequently than in the Aurignacian. The female representations at Laussel are particularly spectacular. They correspond perfectly to the form of numerous, full-figured, female figurines called "Venuses" which have been unearthed in many Gravettian sites across Europe (Sireuil and Tursac in the Dordogne). Gravettian portable art includes animal figurines, finely carved pebbles, and some decorated tools.

Pataud rock-shelter

The Pataud rock-shelter is situated 250 metres downstream from the Cro-Magnon rock-shelter in the village of Les Eyzies, on the left bank of the River Vézère. It was Martial Pataud, a farmer, who discovered the site at the end of the 19th century. However, it was the American prehistorian, Hallam L. Movius, from Harvard University who undertook the scientific dig of this outstanding site. Excavations were launched in 1953 but the main digs were undertaken from 1958 to 1964 and results published in America over a period lasting a quarter of a century. The digs were carried out with remarkable care and attention to detail. Over the last fifteen years, the work has been taken over by the Prehistory laboratory from the Muséum national d'histoire naturelle.

Two large trenches 9.25 m deep flank the main dig. They give an insight into the passage of time and are as easy to "read" as an open book. This is a former shelter which was used as a settlement by prehistoric Man for some fifteen thousand years, from approximately 35,000 years ago. Today, on the site of the dig, the shelter has totally collapsed. Some forty settlements have been found, with remains forming 14 archaeological levels separa-

The Abri Pataud (les Eyzies).

Female silhouette from the Abri Pataud (les Eyzies).
A small block bearing the engraved silhouette (58 mm high) of a woman with atypical proportions was found. According to H. Movius, it came from level 3 (Perigordian VI) – a period which, approximately 21,000 years ago, corresponded to the coldest period of the Würm glaciation. The occupants built a veritable house between the cliff and the blocks of fallen rock. Or at least, this is the interpretation from the numerous artifacts left behind on their living floors which included hearths, the remains of prey, flint tools, objects of adornment, numerous art objects, and even debris from the painted decoration of the rock-shelter (Musée de l'Homme ; copy at the Musée de l'Abri Pataud).

ted by rockfalls – 9 Aurignacian levels, 4 particularly rich Gravettian levels (Perigordian IV, V, VI and VII), one Early Solutrean and the remains of a Solutrean level with laurel leaves.

An abundance of stone and bone artefacts has been uncovered on this site including jewellery and art objects, traces of cave art, and human remains in burial grounds. In all, almost two million objects have been found. This has become the reference site for the beginning of the Early Paleolithic Period.

Developments in the shape of tools over the passage of time reflects cultural changes. A study of even the smallest traces, based on usage, and the spatial distribution of artefacts at a given time sometimes reveal how Man carved a flint implement or how it was used or where they butchered the game that they caught. The aim is to gain greater understanding of Man's lifestyle at that time and to reconstitute the very differing climates that confronted hunters who came here time and again to seek shelter. The climates ranged from very cold (during which vegetation was sparse) to almost temperate climates such as we have today. Even taking account of these more clement periods, the periods of occupation of this site correspond, on average, to the coldest periods of the Quaternary Era.

Behind the farmer's old house, now a research centre, is another very deep shelter. This is, in fact, all that remains of the original shelter which, 35,000 years ago, must have formed a long, narrow platform some one hundred metres in length. On its roof is a superb low-relief carving of a mountain goat. It doubtless dates from the last period of occupation during the Paleolithic period, i.e. during the Solutrean period. The shelter remained in use over successive millennia and has retained traces of this occupation viz. a mediaeval layout as a cave dwelling and an 18th-century front wall (the date "1734" is carved on the lintel above a doorway). It now houses the Pataud rock-shelter museum.

At the base of the cliff, on a level with the main street in Les Eyzies, Mousterians settled on a beach on the banks of the Vézère some 40,000 years ago. The place is called Vignaud.

Laussel

La Grande Beune is a small, babbling brook which flows through a marshy valley. Several kilometers upstream from its junction with La Petite Beune, it passes between two castles. One is medieval and impressive in its austerity, while the second, Laussel, is smaller and less severe. The sites are located 500 meters upstream from Laussel castle and on the same river bank.

The Laussel site was most grandiose in the early 20th century when the woods and copse were still pristine. The Grand Abri stretches 100 meters and rises a dozen meters above the valley floor. It is flanked upstream by a smaller shelter, downstream by the Four (owen) rockshelter, and is situated adjacent to a side vale which climbs abruptly to meet the Department road.

Le Grand Abri was explored in the late 19th century and was later intensively excavated from 1908 to 1914 by Bordeaux native and prehistorian, Doctor Gaston Lalanne. The actual excavation, which was executed by local laborers, foreshadowed the trenches of the world war that would soon begin. Nevertheless, the site proved to be very valuable, both for its volume and the succession of eleven principle archaeological strata which stretched from the Mousterian to the Upper Solutrean. The discovery of depictions of humans in bas-relief underlined the site's importance.

The oldest deposits correspond to diverse facies of the Mousterian, followed by the classic succession of Chatelperronian, typical Aurignacian and Gravettian, as well as several Font Robert points. Finally, in the center of the shelter, two Solutrean levels were found. The superposed strata were five meters thick and were excavated along a 80 meter long trench.

Laussel's renown stem from discoveries made in 1911 and 1912 of five sculpted human representations which seem to be from the Gravettian layer, and consequently date to more than 20,000 years ago.

The most famous, the "Venus with the horn" was made on a stone block of several cubic meters which had fallen at the base of the shelter. It is thus classified as parietal art. The other bas-reliefs art were made on limestone slabs of 40 to 50 centimeters in length and are classified as portable. All were found in a small area of the rockshelter, within a few meters of the "Venus with the horn". The assemblage of art works suggests the existence of a sanctuary or *cella*.

Four of the five bas-reliefs are presently preserved in Bordeaux and exhibited at the Musée d'Aquitaine where

A strange "Venus". This Gravettian statue of a woman measuring 8 cm in height has been carved in the round in some translucent calcite that is amber in colour. It was found in the "Facteur" rock-shelter in Tursac during a dig directed by H. Delporte. The prominent abdomen suggests the late stages of pregnancy but, strangely, the head of the figure has not been carved (Musée des Antiquités nationales).

Hunter or Amazon?
Not far from the 'Venus with the horn' at Laussel, a slab of limestone bears the sculpted image of the profile of a slender person that had long been considered to be male and hence was named "the hunter". It is just as possible to interpret this image as a representation of a young female (Musée d'Aquitaine).

frontal view of nude women with large breasts. In light of certain anatomical features, they probably represent women who have already been through several pregnancies. It is quite possible that the "Venus with the horn" was pregnant, given the size of her abdomen and the gesture of her hand on her stomach.

On the other hand, the profile of the "hunter" has long been described as male. While it has no breasts, it also shows no other male attributes, and it is quite possible that this young individual is female.

The last block is more puzzling. In a deep and wide engraving which was pecked, rather than sculpted, two adjacent persons and inverted head to foot. One of the two is clearly female. Could it be a birthing scene?

Gorge d'Enfer

On the right bank of the Vézère River, the small valley known as the Gorge d'Enfer abruptly ends at the limestone massive which extends from Laugerie-Haute and the Grand Roc to Le Roc de Tayac. Seven prehistoric sites are found here in either caves or under rock-shelters scattered along less than 300 meters. However, this unusual concentration of sites corresponded to a very long stretch of time from the Aurignacian 34,000 years ago to the Upper Magdalenian 12,000 years ago.

On the left flank of the valley, Le Grand Abri is of impressive size at 40 meters deep and about 40 meters long. It was once the opening to a cave which was reshaped by thermoclastic erosion. While it was probably occupied in the Magdalenian, it was emptied of its archaeological filling by saltpeter mining during the French revolution.

Slightly lower and downstream, Abri du Poisson and Abri Lartet were carved out of the stepped hills of a rocky outcrop. The former acquired its name from Edouard Lartet who discovered and excavated the shelter with his friend H. Christy in about 1863. Later in 1918, Peyrony uncovered an Early Aurignacian occupation at Lartet shelter which was characterized by split-based bone

they were donated in 1961 by members of the excavator's family. The fifth bas-relief was sold illegally to the Berlin Museum by a dishonest field director. Possibly destroyed during the second world war, all that remains are the copies at the Musée de l'Homme in Paris and at the Musée d'Aquitaine.

The "Venus with the horn", the "Venus with the gridded hair" and the so-called "Berlin Venus" all depict the

The small valley of Gorge d'Enfer (Les Eyzies).
On the right bank of the Vézère River, slightly upstream from Les Eyzies, the small valley known as the Gorge d'Enfer was inhabited at several periods in prehistory, notably the Aurignacian and the Gravettian.

The hinds of Oreille d'Enfer.
This block depicts a group of four deer without antler (possibly hinds due to their large ears), with juxtaposed limbs which are not in perspective. This is a fragment from the wall of the Oreille d'Enfer (on the left bank of the small Gorge d'Enfer valley) which was removed for questionable preservation reasons (Musée des Eyzies).

The Painted Deer of Abri Vignaud (Les Eyzies).
The large fallen blocks upon which rest the terraces in front of the Pataud museum, once served as a shelter for a Gravettian hunting camp from the Perigordian V and is characterized by Noailles burins. One very large chip of rock was recovered during earlier excavations which showed that the wall was once painted. The piece bears the primitive sketch of a red deer painted in black with elaborate antlers (Musée de l'Abri Pataud).

points and followed by a brief Chatelperronian occupation.

Just next door, Abri du Poisson was not discovered until 1892, and the sculpture of the salmon on the shelter's overhang not until 1912. That same year, the rock surrounding the sculpture was cut away in an initial attempt by the Berlin Museum to purchase the sculpture. However, Peyrony effectively intervened, the venture was abandoned, and the piece is still in place. Following this attempt, in which the sculpture was unfortunately damaged, the rock-shelter was quickly declared a historic monument. The rock-shelter acquired its name from a large meter-long representation of what is incontestably a salmon (perhaps depicted in actual size). It is piked, that is, a male whose lower jaw is curved upward into a hook during the spawning season. The relief is very low and combines raised bas-relief with engraving. The entire object was colored red and some traces are still visible in the grooves of the engravings. Above the fish, a square motif was hatched with seven lines. Below, another relief was carved, but its worn condition makes interpretation of the object difficult. Across from the fish on the same overhang, a negative of a hand stenciled in pale black was discovered several years ago.

The excavation carried out by Peyrony in 1917 and 1918, brought to light two successive occupations of this shelter – one in the Aurignacian as in Abri Lartet, and the second, in the Gravettian. It is reasonable to assume that the sculpture and the painted hand were made during this later period.

Upstream from the Grand Abri, on the same side of the valley, a small cave is preceded by a rocky overhanging. The Oreille-d'Enfer or Les Chênes-Verts cave was excavated intensively and anarchically in the early 20th century. The first "harvest" produced 300 kilograms of flint

A meter-long Salmon.
This sculpture, made on the overhang of Abri du Poisson in the Gorge d'Enfer, represents a meter-long salmon which may be its actual size. It is the only sculpted representation of a fish, an animal rarely depicted in cave art, although it appears more frequently in portable art.

and bones. Two occupations were discovered, one from the Gravettian with Noailles burins and the second from the Solutrean.

On a small flattening of the cave's wall, to the right of the cave's entrance, several engravings were unearthed from beneath the Gravettian level. Thus, the engravings date at least to this period. Two nearly complete animals and the head of a third are represented. The engraving was detached from the wall and moved to Les Eyzies Museum to insure its preservation.

In the cave itself and to the right of the removal scars, six related groups of pecked depressions are near a large central depression surrounded by three smaller ones. These designs are fairly comparable to those found in the Aurignacian of Blanchard, Castanet, and Laussel, and resemble the paw prints of carnivores such as the bear.

The Women of Terme-Pialat (Saint-Avit-Sénieur).
As it was with the Aurignacians, women played a considerable role in the Gravettians' artistic expression. They appeared less frequently in the form of vulvar images. Instead, their abundant silhouettes which were given little detail in the face, arms and legs in bas-relief (at Laussel or Terme-Pialat) and in figurines (at Sireuil and Tursac) are quite famous. They are summarily labelled 'venuses' and were found practically everywhere in Europe. They illustrate the spectacular cultural link that existed among the Gravettians throughout Europe (Musée du Périgord).

Tour 3
From 21,000 to 16,000 years ago
A look at the Solutrean and Early Magdalenian

The days of the Solutreans (18,000-21,000 years ago)

This splendid civilization existed only in a short time and space (in Spain and in the southern half of France between the Loire valley and the Pyrenees). It seemed to have appeared suddenly without direct links to the Gravettian civilization which preceded it in time and possibly originated in the Ardéche region.

Laugerie-Haute

Laugerie-Haute (Upper Laugerie) is a little upriver from Laugerie-Basse (Lower Laugerie) which is how the former acquired its name. The entire cliff faces South-East and is thus well situated. However, from the road which borders the site, neither the shelters not their archaeological remains are visible, since they are masked by an enormous rubble which fell along the cliff's edge during the Magdalenian. Nevertheless, there is a vast living site, 180 meters long and a dozen meters wide, in the excavated area beneath the shelter. It is known that the living site once extended further into the valley under the present day road and beyond.

The site is divided in two sections, Laugerie-Haute East and West, which are located on either side of a talus, upon which the old Chapoulie manor was built back in the 17th century. To the west, below the ruins of the Fournier house, several Neolithic human remains were buried into the Magdalenian layer. This "skeletal shelter" is still private property, while the rest of the site has belonged to the state since 1921.

Lartet and Christy first explored, if not discovered, the site in 1863. Since then, Laugerie-Haute has prompted the interest of a number of archaeologists, enthusiasts, collectors, and profiteers drawn to its rich archaeological material, particularly Solutrean deposits with the laurel leaf – an impressive bifacial flint tool. Fortunately, after assuring that the site was acquired by the state, Peyrony and his son Elie were able to resume their scientific excavation and publish detailed observations in 1938. More recent developments at Laugerie-Haute include, work by Bordes and Ph. Smith which has added to our knowledge of the Upper Paleolithic, and Geneviève Guichard's excavation of the site's eastern section.

Laugerie-Haute rock-shelter (Les Eyzies).
On the right bank of the Vézère, upriver from Les Eyzies, Laugerie-Haute extends 180 meters in length. It was explored in 1863 by Lartet and Christy, but Peyrony is credited with the first significant study of the site. Several successions of civilizations lived here from the Gravettian to the Upper Magdalenian. The different phases are remarkably well represented. At the end of the Middle Magdalenian, the enormous collapse of the shelter's overhang sealed in the existing deposits.

The art of flint knapping.
The people of the Solutrean excelled in the art of flint knapping, producing thin and sharp tools in the shape of laurel leaves with elaborate retouch.

Laugerie-Haute is a very important site in the general assessment of the Upper Paleolithic. Its stratigraphy begins where stratigraphies of earlier occupations at La Ferrassie and Abri Pataud end, and might have been succeeded by Laugerie-Basse in the Middle and Upper Magdalenian, had the latter been properly excavated. Instead, but it is succeeded by La Madeleine for the last three phases (IV, V et VI).

At Laugerie-Haute, forty-two strata and levels were defined including various phases of the Gravettian, the

The engraved bison of La Grèze cave (Marquay).
This bison was engraved using deep but fine lines. It is executed in a primitive evident in its rigid pose in flat profile. The limbs
(one per pair) are stiff and have no hoofs. But some detail began
to appear as well (beard, tail, genitals, relief in the limbs) and
the horns, though they are showing in frontal perspective an
otherwise profile view, seem to be correctly placed below the
nape of the hump. These features indicate that the image is
more developed than those of Pair-non-Pair (Gironde) or Ardèche
caves. This small decorated cave was illuminated by sunlight.
Its entrance overlooks the Grande Beune valley. Early excavations uncovered Magdalenian and Solutrean flint tools
like laurel leaves and shouldered points. The still
rather rudimentary form of the animals, engraved
in flat profile, the presence of certain anatomical
details, and the absence of archaeological artifacts
predating the Solutrean, place this small engraving
in the Solutrean.

A lignite pendant. Le Fourneau du Diable (Bourdeilles).
This pendant is one of the rare portable art objects from the Solutrean. Made from lignite, a rare stone, it bears the engraved silhouette of a fairly rudimentary deer. The choice of material
denotes the Solutreans' interest in rare minerals. It is also known
that they collected small shiny pebbles (Musée des Eyzies).

Solutrean, and the first half of the Magdalenian. The Magdalenians V and VI were observed in old collections, but no objects are left in place. The sequence of intensive occupations of this vast rock-shelter represents a period of some 10,000 years and corresponds to a succession of several climatic phases which were meticulously analyzed by Henri Laville.

Laugerie-Haute is less rich in art objects than sites like Laugerie-Basse or La Madeleine, but some of them are of singular interest. The Final Gravettian or Perigordian VII produced a large 30 centimeter long gneiss pebble. Deeply incised groups of lines extending in several directions, forming puzzling motifs, are portrayed which must have been difficult to carve on the rock's hard surface. From the same period, a pierced baton ("baton percé") made from reindeer antler bears the engraved and light relief depictions of facing mammoths like those found on the walls of Rouffignac cave. A sculpted piece of reindeer antler from the Early Solutrean which, according to Bordes, bears the head and body of a feline, was an exceptional find for this period. The backdirt from Hauser's excavations yielded a limestone sculpture of the head of an Ovibos, or musk ox, with distinctive horns bent to the forehead. The musk ox is rarely portrayed in prehistoric art.

An ibex sculpted in bas-relief (Abri Pataud, Les Eyzies).
In view of its style and the laurel leaves found on the ground beneath it, this ibex is definitely Solutrean. It was discovered in 1986 and today takes its place among the most exquisite works of prehistoric art. It was made in a similar fashion to the sculptures in Roc de Sers and Fourneau du Diable, and may date to 18,000 or 19,000 years ago. Note, however, that the rear limbs are simply juxtaposed and are not depicted on separate planes and in perspective like the forward limbs. This male alpine ibex (*Capra ibex*) is readily identified by its horns, (the position of the left horn is unusual but not unique in prehistoric art). The small head, large belly, and short and animated limbs are in keeping with the style at Lascaux This splendid sculpture was discovered on the ceiling of a rock-shelter, which, in the 18th century, was transformed into a wine-cellar and converted today into a site museum. This cellar was part of a farm built into the cliff in the small town of Les Eyzies. The Prehistoric site of Abri Pataud is located beneath the former Pataud barn and the old farm house currently serves as a research center.

The Sculpted Block from Le Fourneau du Diable (Bourdeilles).
This nearly half a cubic meter block is sculpted in bas-relief with animal shapes – two aurochs to the right and another oblique one in the center, as well as a barely visible horse further to the left. Other traces of animal forms or rough-outs are found in the upper right corner, and vulvar signs in the laurel are found in the lower right corner. The assemblage of animals must have been colored in red ochre, since a few traces still remain. What is particularly remarkable is the respect for natural perspective which situates the two aurochs on the right, as well as the right and left limbs of the lower auroch, on two separate planes. By removing the rock surrounding the image, the animal's volume is accentuated in bas-relief against the background. The separation, however, was never completed and a small section of rock is still intact between the two aurochs' heads (Musée des Eyzies).

Artisans and talented artists

The Solutreans were very skilled artisans and artists. They made high quality flint tools retouched on all surfaces. This technique lent considerable beauty to implements like unifaced points, laurel leaves, shouldered points, and willow leaf points. They also invented a tool used in life's daily routines: the eyed bone needle.

The Solutreans were also fine artists. They decorated small caves in the Ardèche Gorge with engravings and drawings (Chabot and Bidon), using red and black pigments. They also made use of graphic artifices that were to become commonplace during the Lascaux period (e.g. cattle horns in twisted perspective).

The Solutrean Period in South-Western France left a particularly large number of rock-shelters decorated with bas-reliefs, although the art work has unfortunately been badly preserved here. The roof of the intact section of the Pataud Shelter, with its carved mountain goat, is an exception to this. In Le Fourneau-du-Diable near Bourdeilles and Le Roc-de-Sers (Charente) between Brantôme and Angoulême, large areas of rock have been carved in Solutrean shelters.

The cattle in Le Fourneau-du-Diable are highly characteristic of the Solutrean period style in this area, with

A portable light in the Magdalenian period.
This block of limestone measuring some 20 cm along each side was hollowed out to be used as a tallow lamp as is obvious from the blackened, rubefied traces in the base and on the edges. Gabillou Cave in Sourzac (Musée d'Aquitaine).

One horse among hundreds (Lascaux).
This horse was engraved in thin angular lines using a sharp flint tool. It displays a Lascaux style with its small head, large belly, short and animated limbs, rounded hoofs beneath dew-claws, and fetlock hairs.

their small heads, prominent stomach and short legs (and, on one of them, an ear placed in the back of the neck). Natural perspective has been maintained and two aurochs to the right have been superimposed over two levels. The animals carved in bas-relief in Le Roc-de Sers are comparable to them. In technical terms, these carvings represent a blossoming of Gravettian artistry in this region and, stylistically, they are the precursors of the great artistic skill which, one thousand years later, was to give rise to Lascaux, the work of early Magdalenians.

A comfortable place to live

Situated in the site of Fourneau du Diable and dating to the Late Solutrean, a remarkable living structure was uncovered. It consisted of a hut with a square base, surrounded by stones. The climate of this period was harsh, cold, and dry, particularly in the early and late periods of the Solutrean, interrupted by temperate, more humid climatic (one of which is best known as the Laugerie interstadial). Reindeer were abundant in the beginning of this period, and were followed later by ibexes and Solutré horses. With the exception of Solutré in Saone-et-Loire, the major sites of this time period are located in the Dordogne. These include Laugerie-Haute, Fourneau du Diable, Jean-Blancs, and Abri Pataud. Few objects were decorated during this period, except in Parpallo near Valencia, Spain, which produced engravings on plaquettes of stone from the Gravettian to the Middle Magdalenian.

The Badegoulians and the first Magdalenians (17,000 years ago)

The beginning of the great phase of the Upper Paleolithic is marked by the abundant bone industry and the quality and diversity of parietal and portable art. This is the period of Lascaux. The Magdalenian culture extended throughout Europe, but in the early stages, it was restricted to the French Southwest and to a large site in Spain (La Parpallo near Valencia). The early sites were few in number and included Laugerie-Haute and Badegoule in the Dordogne (where the culture is sometimes referred to as Badegoulian), and Le Placard in Charente. The Early Magdalenian is not represented in the eponymous site of La Madeleine.

A separate culture between the Solutrean and the Magdalenian

Today, many authors believe the Badegoulian culture, which emerged at the start of the Magdalenian, constituted an independent culture and a product of the Final Solutrean. It is characterized by a low number of backed blades and bladelets, an abundance of retouched flake scrapers, thick notched burins, and numerous flake perforators. The bases of the bone points have single bevels and hafting striations. Some bone implements are thick, and reindeer antler was worked using primitive percussion methods not practiced in the Magdalenian that followed.

The first true Magdalenian

The first Magdalenians continued to use the same basic tools of the Upper Paleolithic: blades, burins, and end-scrapers. But they also made dihedral burins, backed blades, small perforators, end-scrapers on unretouched blades, and composite tools (end-scraper-burins, etc.). Bone points had thick, conical bases and were decorated with a few engraved lines sometimes in the shape of stars or enclosed chevrons (as in Lascaux). Harpoons had not yet been invented. The climate was mild 17,000 years ago in the Lascaux interstadial but became cold and dry soon thereafter.

The conquest of the underground world

One of the most remarkable events in the early Magdalenian was the invention or at least the expanded use of the tallow lamp – a natural stone with a slight depression or a carefully carved stone lamp made to form a receptacle. This event gave humans access to the underground world, where they decorated deep-set sanctuaries. This marked the beginnings of a Magdalenian artistic explosion, and soon meant an increase in the number of cave sanctuaries and art objects. However, apart from Lascaux – which was both a training workshop and a masterpiece – few decorated caves date back to this period, although one could cite Villars and Gabillou which resemble Lascaux in their style. From this time forward, underground sanctuaries increased in number.

The Lascaux sanctuary (Montignac) The prehistoric Sistine Chapel

The entrance to the cave sanctuary of Lascaux was blocked shortly after the cave was decorated 17,000 years ago by the first Magdalenians. This opening, which was reopened by a fallen tree, was discovered on September 8, 1940 by a young Montignac boy, Marcel Ravidat, when his dog had fallen into its depths. Marcel returned four days later with three friends (C. Agniel, S. Coencas, and J. Marsal) to widen the hole.

Lascaux cave is only 150 meters long, but its passageways are wide and high. The Hall of Bulls and the Axial Gallery were painted on hard, white, calcite walls. The rest of the cave (The Passageway, The Nave, The Apse, The Pit, The Chamber of Felines) was primarily decorated with engravings, and mixed paintings/engravings and paintings on yellowed limestone and sandstone surfaces.

Lascaux's floor had only one archaeological layer. Its contents included artist tools, flint and bone tools, objects of adornment, lamps, the remains of meals, pollens, charcoal, etc. These vestiges allow us to reconstitute the lives of those who frequented the cave and to date the works on the cave's walls. Methodical excavations would have produced better results, but the floor was summarily removed from the cave without scientific control during initial cleaning efforts.

Lascaux cave was a sanctuary. The organization and quality of its images, as well as the objects abandoned by those who frequented the cave prove that this was not the lair of some magician but rather a kind of cathedral devoted to one of prehistory's religions. Lascaux' artists were professionals who performed a service for the group and for the faith of its members.

The tourism generated by this decorated cave was formidable and almost resulted in the cave's destruction. Pollution, caused in part by the artificial recirculation of air, spread a green algae on the cave walls. It required that the cave be disinfected. The carbon dioxide, heat, and water vapors, brought in by tens of thousands of visitors each year (120,000 in 1962!), may have proliferated the opaque film of white calcite crystals which eventually covered the paintings. The dangers of this white disease caused the cave to be closed to tourism and attempts were made to recreate the microclimate which

A "very Lascaux" horse (called "Chinese horse") (Axial Gallery, Lascaux).

This 1.40 meter-long horse is very characteristic of the conventions of Lascaux artists: the small head, ballooned abdomen, short and animated limbs, the double line on the shoulder, the flat M-shaped coat, and dew-claws over rounded hoofs. The left limbs of the animal are separated from the body by a space which displays their position on a different plane. The raised mane, the light beard, as well as the coat and silhouette of the animal in general resemble the present day Przewalski's horse which is indigenous to Asia.

A perfect copy: Lascaux II.

Since the preservation of Lascaux forced it to close its doors to tourism, two facsimiles were built. The first used actual size photograph-images which were applied to the reconstituted walls of the Hall of Bulls (Musée des Antiquités Nationales). The second was more ambitious and consisted of a copy of the Hall of Bulls and the Axial Gallery built underground near the original cave.

In single file (The Nave, Lascaux).

Five painted deer heads, each a meter high, form a frieze in The Nave. The artists must have climbed atop the talus to gain access to this surface. The frieze consists of a group of fairly mature red deer depicted as one might have observed them in nature. The antlers are displayed in a conventional fashion, one before the other. Even the ears are depicted in a classical Lascaux style where one ear is tucked against the nape and the other against the side of the neck. The first four were drawn in black using manganese dioxide, while the last is maroon and was made using cave clay. The people of Lascaux did not eat these deer. Instead, they preferred reindeer which, save one, are not represented in this cave. An incomplete horse, which is difficult to discern, and a group of dots complement this composition. Though still unproven, the whole is thought to represent a river crossing. The reproduction of this frieze is on exhibit at Le Thot in Thonac, the Musée d'Aquitaine in Bordeaux, and the American Museum of Natural History in New York.

had preserved the art works for the past seventeen millennia.

The future will tell whether this treatment has been effective but, since 1983, a copy (Lascaux II) has shown visitors most of what people once saw in the original cave. Lascaux II is a ferrous cement shell shaped and built to the dimensions of the galleries in the cave itself. The figures and signs visible in the original cave have been painted on its walls as accurately as possible.

Lascaux II provided an opportunity to try out the techniques used by the original artists. They created their works using manganese dioxide (black) and natural ochres (yellows, browns and purples). The bright reds may have been obtained by a process of oxidation. The pigments were applied using the fingers, brushes made of animal or plant fibres, or wads of fur or fibres. The outlines, some of which are very sharp, were obtained using skin stencils. It is not known for sure whether the pigments were blown onto the surface through a hollow bone or straight from the mouth. This would be a laborious process on large surfaces and too imprecise for small areas. It would also have a number of unpleasant side-effects for artists painting on the roof. Pigments came from "pencils" of ochre or manganese which were either used

FROM TOP TO BOTTOM:

Horses, deer and aurochs in the Hall of Bulls (Lascaux).
The association of a large bovine and several smaller horses is
a common theme in Lascaux Art, and no doubt filled with sym-
bolism. Unfortunately the meaning of this mythogram was lost.
The contour lines of the bull are thick and retraced in red around
the horns and withers. Near its forehead, lies a symmetrical
pattern of dots and short lines.

The resin on flint implements at Lascaux.
Some flint tools still bear the remnants of an adhesive on the
side or face that served to secure a haft (in grey on the drawing). It was not possible to analyze this adhesive in more
detail, although it was probably made of powdered ochre and
resin. The ochre was identified, but the resin, like all organic
material, had decomposed and was not preserved. Still, this
discovery gives us a clearer idea of how prehistoric humans
used the tiny flint blades: they were hafted (Institut de Paléon-
tologie humaine).

A sculpted, polished, and engraved, pink sandstone, lamp (The
Pit, Lascaux).
This splendid object was found at the bottom of The Well. A
small depression in the lamp still contains some decomposed
matter. This tallow lamp was used like our old oil lamps. Other
lamps discovered in Lascaux include a lamp carved out of a
limestone block and over one hundred lamps consisting of unal-
tered, flat, or slightly concave stones. Experimentation demons-
trated that these stones, when supplied with a small dried-twig
fire and a piece of tallow, worked like a candle in which the
small fire would melt the fat upon contact. The charcoal would
soak in the melted grease and from then on act as the wick.
The amount of light given off by such a lamp, with one or several wicks, is equivalent to one of our candles. The lamps handle
(for which the pink sandstone originated in nearby Corrèze),
bears patterned signs which are unique to Lascaux (Musée des
Antiquités nationales).

The same signs appear on one of the many bone points found
in the cave's sediments as well as on the cave walls. This proves
that the objects found in the cave's only archeological layer do
indeed belong to the artists of Lascaux cave which dates to
17,000 years ago – the Early Magdalenian (Musée des Eyzies).

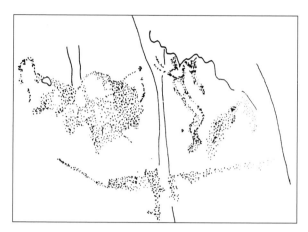

In Villars as in Lascaux: a pictogram.

Here in Villars, a person holds its arms out in front. Calcite formation stands between the animal and the human figure. Another passes through the bison's back. Villars cave, near Brantôme, is an immense labyrinth, more than 10 kilometers long, with a great many concretions on its walls. In 1953, the SpeleoClub of Périgueux discovered the entrance. The paintings, which were found in 1958, are analogous in style to the images in Lascaux. However, they are fewer in number and often covered by a veil of calcite which gives the black manganese lines, (used to draw the images), a steely blue tint. This too was a sanctuary and as in Lascaux, the scene of the human confronting a bison was made on the most remote panel of the cave.

Object of adornment in the floor of Lascaux.

The people of Lascaux had a taste for adornment. Sixteen whole shells were discovered in the archaeological deposits. Three of them could be suspended on a string. Some originated from the Atlantic coast; other possibly came from the Mediterranean, and still others from the Tertiary layers of the Aquitaine or Tourane. This Sipho was pierced for suspension. It originated at the seashore and still carries red ochre in its spires – a pigment that was probably used to tan hides or to paint the skin of the man or woman who wore this gem. Lascaux even yielded a less exotic predecessor to our costume-jewelry: an oval pebble transformed into a shell by the addition of a few engraved lines which simulate spires (Musée des Eyzies).

directly on the rock or scraped to produce a coloured powder set onto the wall of rock thanks to the lime-bearing water.

Art in Lascaux

The decoration in Lascaux is particularly structured; nothing is left to chance. It is like a cathedral, with themes carefully distributed across the available space and completed by a language based on geometric symbols whose meaning is still unclear to us.

The art in Lascaux is very unusual. Animal anatomy and behaviour have been carefully observed but the outlines have been systematically misshapen, in a conventional style that is specific to this site. The hand of the artist has corrected and transformed what the eye of the hunter has seen. This unusual art succeeded the more rudimentary graphics of the Aurignacians and Gravettians and preceded the more realistic, and classical, work of the Middle and Upper Magdalenians. Lascaux is the oldest of the Magdalenian cave sanctuaries. It is also the most unusual, most beautiful and best known. Among the explosion of art in the Magdalenian period, Lascaux appears as a "trial run" and as a "consummate masterpiece" produced by the artists, like a dazzling explosion that, for once, opens the fireworks display instead of ending it.

There are three types of symbol in Lascaux – "full" signs, most of them large rectangles divided into sections, like the famous "coats-of-arms"; "thin" signs which consist of sticks expanding laterally and ranging in form from a star with six branches centred on one point to a St. Andrew's Cross, lines bearing several barbs or chevrons imbricated one in the other; and, finally, punctuation marks in the form of one or two lines. One last category of sign seen in Lascaux deserves a special mention – the signs shaped like a club, usually only seen in the caves in Ariège or Spain that were decorated some time after Lascaux. The meaning of all these signs, a veritable mystery "language", remains unknown.

In the Middle and Upper Magdalenian, a few thousand years after Lascaux, art became much more realistic and less unusual than the work seen in Lascaux, but the signs nevertheless remained frequent and enigmatic.

A strange story (Lascaux, The Pit).
As the exception to the rule, this scene seems to tell a story. An eviscerated bull, with its intestines hanging, charges into a simple stick-figure human with a bird's head, four fingers on each hand, and an erect penis. Although, the animal is stiff, an unnaturally lowered head and a tail whipping about in the air give it some animation. Below, a bird seems to be perched upon a spear thrower and a barbed line may represent a bone point. Further to the left, stands a woolly rhinoceros across from which a horse was drawn. The bottom of The Pit contained a variety of objects, including lamps – one made of pink sandstone –, bone points, flint tools and pigments. Cave art, without exception, consists of juxtaposed images and signs, without any clear link between them. Narrative scenes, like this one (and in Villars cave and at the site of Roc du Sers), are very rare. Many facsimiles have been made of this famous panel and are currently on display to the public, notably at Le Thot in Thonac.

Paleolithic Art is not anecdotal. The animals, human figures (these are rarer) and signs that form the art works in these cave sanctuaries, do not illustrate a story. They are mythograms, whose meaning has been lost, in the absence of any information handed down by the person who originally explained them. A few pictograms are still comprehensible today e.g. the scenes showing a man and an ox (Lascaux, Villars, Le Roc de Sers), mountain goats locked in combat (Lascaux), or mammoths (Rouffignac), the two bison placed rump to rump in Lascaux, or a few other ethological scenes which show that the cave artists were also hunters, with excellent knowledge of the anatomy and behaviour of animals.

The artistry of the great hunters of France and Spain, the art work visible in rock-shelters and caves, died out some 10,000 years ago. It came to light again elsewhere in Europe, on rocks in the open air (Arctic, Alps, Spanish Levant etc.) where it was often more diagrammatic than the work dating from our Paleolithic age and full of representations of human figures.

From 16,000 to 13,000 years ago
The Middle Magdalenian

It has become conventional to speak of the Middle Magdalenian which corresponds to stages III and IV of Breuil's subdivisions. Others would prefer to link stage III to the Lower Magdalenian and stage IV to the Upper Magdalenian. This period is marked by a cold phase which lasted two thousand years, followed by a relatively milder climate. In the first phase, reindeer abound along with horses and saïga antelopes across a steppic grassy landscape. In the second phase, horses increased in number, while the antelope population decreased radically or disappeared. The climate became milder and more humid. Tree cover increased and even included deciduous trees.

The Magdalenian stone tool assemblage was fairly unremarkable with the usual procession of end-scrapers and burins which were often either combined on the same blade or associated with other tools. Tiny retouched bladelets were quite numerous and were sometimes either denticulated or triangular. Bone and reindeer antler indus-

tries are the key distinguishing features. Stage III is characterized by bone points which are often short and thick, with a single bevel, and generally with a longitudinal grove in the back. Semi-cylindrical antler segments also emerged at this time, often with either no decoration, or decorated with incised geometric signs. One also finds pierced batons, smoothing tools, notched bone, needles, etc.

In stage IV, bone points with single or double bevels, while sometimes striated, no longer bear dorsal groves. Antler segments are engraved or decorated with motifs in relief. Reindeer antler points also appear with lateral notches. These are often described as harpoon prototypes. One also finds small, thin, perforated bone disks bearing geometric decorations or animal representations. Hooked spear throwers were made from reindeer antler or ivory, and were occasionally decorated with impressive full-round animal sculpture. The number of engravings on bone, ivory, reindeer antler, stones, pebbles, or plaquettes increased significantly in this period.

While defined at Laugerie-Haute, the Magdalenian III is also present at Cap Blanc, Reverdit, Raymonden, Gabillou and in some open-air sites in the Isle Valley. The Magdalenian IV was present in the lower stratum of the eponymous site, and at Laugerie-Basse and Raymonden.

Cap Blanc

The abri du Cap Blanc is located at mid-slope on the right bank of the Grande Beune valley, almost directly across from the powerful Commarque castle, the setting for Robert Merle novel *Malevil*. It was not until the beginning of the 20th century that an excavator from the Laussel site, standing at the base of a small cliff, noticed a small crevice – a sign of a possible rock-shelter – and undertook an excavation on behalf his director, Dr. G. Lalanne. The operation was completed rather quickly. From September to December 1909, the entire site – fifteen meters long and three or four meters wide – had been completely excavated. When they reached the rock-shelter's rear wall, the excavators noticed the sculptures consisting of an animal frieze in high and low-relief.

This monumental assembly is unique in the Périgord. No equivalent exists for this period, except at the abri du Roc aux Sorciers at Angle-sur-l'Anglin in Vienne. The composition is divided into two panels. The panel on the left is nine meters long and is located in the deepest recesses of the rock-shelter, while the second, further to the right, is four meters long and located in part on the ceiling of the rock-shelter's overhang.

Among the fourteen recorded animal represented, six

Horses emerging from the wall.

No one knows why the Magdalenians, who lived in Cap Blanc, sculpted this extraordinary frieze of horses on the wall of their rock-shelter. While it is believed that art had a magical or religious significance, it was placed here in a living site itself for all to see.

are horses. All of them face to the right, save the most spectacular one in the center of the shelter which measures two meters in length. In two cases, a superposition of animals occurs where the head of the first is on the rump of the next. Three bison are also depicted among which one bison head was sculpted on a horse's head. A fourth bison was sculpted on a large collapsed block beneath the rock-shelter, now preserved at the Musée d'Aquitaine. A few other animals were more difficult to classify and are best left unidentified. Traces of red ochre are still visible in some places, which leads us to believe that this frieze was once colored.

A study of the lithic and bone industries from Cap Blanc, preserved at the Musée de l'Homme and at the Musée d'Aquitaine, attributes the two principal layers of the site to the Middle Magdalenian (Breuil's Magdalenian III). It was during this period that the parietal frieze

A carved block of stone.
At Cap Blanc, a bison facing right was sculpted on a large slab of limestone that had slid away and lay at the base of the shelter's wall, in front of the recess located to the right, in the very heart of the archaelogical layer. Three other small bison are sculpted on the rock face.

A bison rock-shelter.
Here in Reverdit, three bison were sculpted for every horse, while at Cap Blanc the horse to bison ratio is six to two or three. Nevertheless, both sites are from the same period in the Magdalenian.

The famous "hut" of La Mouthe (Les Eyzies).
Despite the nickname that was ascribed to this engraved and painted design, it is unlikely that it represents a prehistoric hut. The artists from this period did not portray objects or landscapes, only animals, humans, and puzzling geometric signs. This 'hut' is one of these signs and is probably but attributed to the famous tectiform signs. These ethnic indicators are characteristic of caves in the Les Eyzies region from the Middle Magdalenian. The meaning of most of these signs is still a mystery.

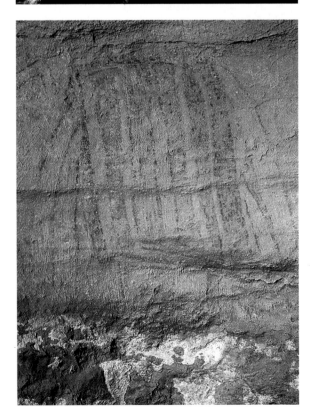

was produced. However, there is some indication based on old collections, an excavation by Peyrony, and later from one of our own excavations, that the site was also occupied briefly during the Upper Magdalenian.

A human burial was discovered at the very base of the archaeological filling. It contained the skeleton of a young woman, about twenty years in age, who was laid on the left side in a flexed position. The heels almost touch the pelvis, and the right hand covers the face. Three stone slabs were placed on the body. The skeleton currently on exhibit in the rock-shelter is in a different place from where it was discovered for the skeleton itself is a modern reconstruction, since the original was sold by the owner of the site to the Museum of Natural History, Chicago. Thus, all under one rock-shelter, Cap Blanc shows a direct association among daily routine, funerary ritual, and splendid works of art which were possibly linked to the religion and rituals of the Magdalenian people.

Abri Reverdit

In the Vallon des Roches in Sergeac, below Castelmerle, two rock-shelters were occupied during the Magdalenian. The first, La Souquette, is located on the left slope of the vallon and faces the Vézère River. The second, Abri

Reverdit, is on the same side of the valley, only 300 meters upstream. The latter derives its name from Alain Reverdit, an employee of Administration des Tabacs, who discovered it in 1875. Beneath the rock-shelter, which at the time was used as a stable or manger, he excavated what was left of the archeological filling. Later from 1911 to 1914, Franck Delage reopened the excavation in front of the rock-shelter, recognizing that the prehistoric occupation had also extended towards the valley floor. The two recognized layers of archeological deposits were defined as Magdalenian III, just as at Cap Blanc. It wasn't until around 1923 that Marcel Castanet, the owner of the site, discovered the sculptures along the overhang of the rock-shelter. In contrast to Cap Blanc, these sculptures are quite poorly preserved and occupy only a small section of the wall to the right, where a horse, two bison and the back of a third are portrayed.

In the left (or upriver) section of the site, a sloping talus abuts against the cliff face outside the rock-shelter and covers the remains of recently excavated archaeological strata. Several hearths appear in the control section, at the base of which another hearth, surrounded by large river cobblestones and placed on their sides in an oval formation, was uncovered.

The bison discovery: La Mouthe (Les Eyzies).
This engraved bison, depicted in great detail and in normal perspective, was the first engraved image to be discovered by G. Berthoumeyrou on April 11, 1895. It is located 100 meters from the entrance, on a wall of a small chamber surrounded by nine other bison, two ibexes, one deer, and various other vestiges. The style of these images is Lascaux type Magdalenian. The horns are longer than in today's bison and are shown at three-quarters perspective. Closer to the entrance, a small chamber features more rudimentary, if not more ancient, animals.

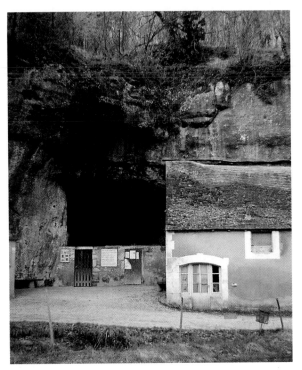

Far end a valley.

The residents of a small farm built a stable in a cavity in the cliffs of the Vallon des Combarelles. From here, a narrow, long and winding chamber plunges underground and is covered with dozens of prehistoric engravings.

Les Combarelles

"Hurrah! As discoveries go, this one made of an immense engraved cave is big enough for both Capitan and myself. It is over 300 meters long and more than half its length consists of animal engravings, particularly horses, but also antelopes, reindeer, mammoths, and ibexes. It is just a dream come true. We happened upon it by chance, just as one might stumble upon something in the road. It is just too good to be true, especially when one has worked so hard for so long. I've traced 18 animals, and some of them are splendid indeed but are covered by a stalagmite film. Alas, there were far too many images, rather than not enough, and a number of beautiful heads are obscured. The profiles of some images were also outlined in black. This find is sure to shock the world of prehistoric art."

This enthusiastic excerpt was taken from a letter written by the young Abbé Breuil to a friend and fellow school-mate from the seminary, Abbé Bouyssonie from Brive. It was written shortly after Breuil, along with Louis Capitan and Denis Peyrony, discovered the cave in Les Combarelles on September 8, 1901. The discovery was a significant one indeed, since only five decorated caves were known to exist at this time. Curiously, some archaeo-

logists were indifferent and even hostile toward the concept of cave art. The great antiquity of human beings had long been established, and numerous works of art had been unearthed and recognized as prehistoric. Still, many could not imagine that "primitives" were capable of penetrating the cave depths to practice their art.

The discoveries at La Mouthe in 1895 and at Pair-non-Pair (Gironde) in 1896 probably already planted the seed of doubt in the minds of the skeptics. The discovery of Les Combarelles, and of Font-de-Gaume several days later, was decisive. In May 1902, E. Cartailhac made honorable amends by publishing his "*mea culpa d'un sceptique*" in the periodical *L'Anthropologie*. In August of the same year, a committee of specialists visited the three decorated caves in Les Eyzies and acknowledged the prehistoric age of the images. Numerous other discoveries made in the ensuing years revealed several new caves in the Périgord, the Pyrenees, and in Spain.

The existence of Les Combarelles was known prior to 1901. From 1891 to 1894, prehistorian E. Rivière had already excavated a rich site located near the entrance to the cave and the right gallery, called Combarelles II, where several engravings were found in 1934. The main gallery, Combarelles I, is 240 meters long in its upper section. It is a narrow passage way with eleven bends and averages a meter in width but widens periodically at elbow level. After its discovery access was facilitated by lowering the floor, whereas originally, one was forced to crawl on a stalagmite floor filled with concretions to reach the engravings.

The diversity of fauna represented illustrates perfectly animal life in the Magdalenian. Included are rhinoceroses, bears, felines, and wolves. Horses were by far the most numerous with one hundred, and, according to Breuil, constitute a third of the engraved animal images. The next in order of frequency were bison, aurochs, bears, reindeer, mammoths, and deer.

Many human or anthropomorphic representations are intermixed with animal figures. A few very stylized depictions resemble the engravings at Lalinde or at Couze from the Upper Magdalenian. To this assortment, one must add signs, especially the tectiforms, the same as those found in Bernifal, Font-de-Gaume, and Rouffignac. Based on their style, these works appear to stem from the Magdalenian, or more specifically the Middle Magdalenian; this according to A. Leroi-Gourhan, who did not exclude the possibility that some may be more recent and contemporaneous with engravings from Teyjat and Limeuil (Magdalenian V and VI respectively). In fact, a section of the layer excavated in 1973 in the chamber's entrance provided two carbon 14 dates. The oldest date was 11,730 B.C., while the youngest was 9,430 B.C.

Feline Number 52.

Soon after the discovery of Les Combarelles in 1901, Abbé Breuil committed himself to the task of tracing the cave's wall engravings. He succeeded in distinguishing 191 engravings depicted in 105 groups. Group number 52 associates a feline (the details of the head shown here), one upright rhinoceros, and a second depicted upside down and inverted head to foot with the first, surely a mysterious confrontation.

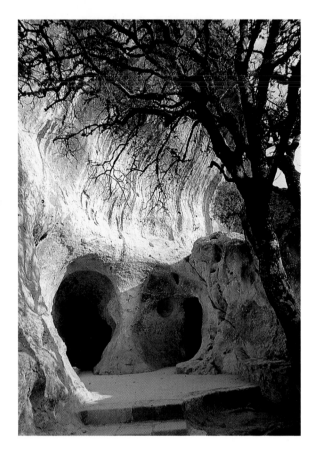

The Entrance to the Sanctuary.
The residents of Les Eyzies have always known the grotte de Font-de-Gaume. They visited it frequently and unknowingly carved their names over the prehistoric drawings that went unnoticed. Just four days after the discovery of Les Combarelles, Denis Peyrony, then a grade school teacher, decided to return to Font-de-Gaume. There, he discovered and recognized the engravings and paintings covering the cave walls. The right gallery leads to the Magdalenian sanctuary, while the one to the left dead ends after a few meters.

Font-de-Gaume

In H. Breuil's words, Font-de-Gaume deserves to be ranked among the "giants" in cave art. While the frescoes covering the walls of the main chamber are not as bright as in Lascaux, and while they have sometimes been defaced by graffiti or covered by a veil of calcite, the high quality of the work emerges in the technique and style. The locals had known of the cave's existence for some time. As Breuil amusingly explained, the cave was a favorite meeting place for young adults on their rendez-vous. The grade school teacher, Denis Peyrony, knew of the cave as well, and three days after an expedition to Les Combarelles, he decided to return there to look at the walls with new eyes. He was the first to see these "paintings of exquisite beauty" and eagerly alerted Breuil and Capitan who arrived on September 21st. For months, even years, Breuil regularly returned to Les Eyzies where, aided at times by Peyrony, he went about recording the paintings and engravings at Font-de-Gaume and Les Combarelles. The monograph on the former was richly illustrated with colors and published in 1910. The latter was published in 1924.

The cave was carved out of a large limestone outcrop, five hundred meters along the flank of the vale of Font-de-Gaume which opens on the left bank of La Beune. Starting from a sheltered porch that was remodeled in the Middle Ages, the main gallery is 120 meters long and noticeably narrow. Three galleries split off its right wall, one of which one leads to the outside. The main paintings and engravings are located in the second half of the main gallery, just before the narrowing passage named "the Rubicon", and continue along the high but narrow passage way until it dead ends. Several representations are also present in the second gallery and still others in the third.

Unlike Les Combarelles cave which was dedicated to horses, Font-de-Gaume cave was devoted to bison. H. Breuil counted 80 bison, 40 horses, 23 mammoths, 17 reindeer and deer, 8 aurochs, 4 goats, 2 felines, 1 wolf, 1 bear, and 1 human. To this one should add numerous signs, including 19 tectiforms and four negative (or stenciled) hands executed in color. The paintings are of exceptional quality. They are often bichrome or polychrome and superimposed upon a previously engraved representation of part or all of the animal. Time and time again, especially in the case of bison, the natural relief of the cave wall was used to suggest the volume of certain body parts like the head, hump, or limbs. The animals are not randomly distributed. Some are associated in pairs such as two facing reindeer in a touching scene of loving affection. Others are portrayed in single file or organized in compositions. Some species occupy special positions. High on the cave wall, a wolf faces the intersection of the main and third gallery; a rhinoceros was painted in the last gallery, and an engraved feline at the very narrow end of the same passageway faces a group of horses. A study of the styles and superpositions shows that the work was completed in several stages; one, more or less contemporaneous with Lascaux in the Early Magdalenian, and the other, in the later Magdalenian as found at Les Combarelles, Bernifal, and Rouffignac.

Bernifal

Bernifal cave faces a hillside on the left bank of the Petite Beune, just downstream from the Vieil Mouly manor and former mill, on the road from Les Eyzies to Sarlat.

In 1902, Denis Peyrony penetrated the cave through a small opening in the ceiling. He was not the first to pass this way, as testified by the graffiti made on the walls prior to his discovery of the paintings and engravings.

The cave was composed of two main halls, separated by a very low and narrow passageway. Several small galleries which lead off from the second hall, also conceal engravings and paintings in passages which are at times very narrow and barely accessible.

As in Rouffignac (but to a lesser degree), Bernifal is a mammoth cave. Mammoths constitute more than half of the 50 recorded animal representations. Most are engraved and the rest are painted including one which one deserves to be ranked among the best of the Rouffignac mammoths. Here, one finds a sense of style if not skill. Eight horses, including one ass, seven bovines (bison and aurochs), and two deer complete the list of animals featured in the cave, which also has nine unidentifiable animals. In one gallery, the natural relief in the cave wall resembles the profile of a human head. A few engraved lines made by prehistoric humans outline the nose, eye, and mouth.

Bernifal is also a tectiform cave. In the Périgord, these signs bear a strong resemblance to a drawing of a house with a gable roof, but it is unlikely that they represented living structures. There are thirteen such signs here. Twelve are engraved and one is painted using a series of small,

Another tectiform sign was painted in the Bernifal Cave. In normal light (above), one can discern the general shape of the painting, but when photographed on infra-red film (below), it is clear that the painting was made using a very organized series of small, juxtaposed, and evenly distributed dots.

juxtaposed dots. The engraved tectiforms are sometimes isolated, other times in pairs, and at times associated with mammoths. One animal that is absent here is the rhinoceros, while it is usually a counterpart to the mammoth in other decorated caves in the region like Les Combarelles and Font-de-Gaume. There is at least one hand stenciled in black.

Rouffignac

Rouffignac cave, also known as the grotte du Cluzeau, Cro de Granville, or grotte de Miremont, formed in a flint rich limestone hill, on the banks of the vale of La Binche, just 5 kilometer as the crow flies from the Vézère River. It would require many pages to recount the history of this cave which goes back to the year 1575. Rouffignac was the subject of what is probably the oldest known description of a decorated cave. In his *Cosmographie Universelle de tout le monde*, F. Belleforest mentioned "paintings and drawings of animals". Over the last century, it was described in tourist guides as a center of interest. However, the discovery of prehistoric images dates only to 1956, when Ch. Plassard and two Pyrenees prehistorians, L.-R. Nougier and R. Robert, visited the cave and found these drawings.

Currently, 226 animal and four human representations have been recorded. This "cave of one hundred mammoths", as it is called in the tourist guides, in fact contains 158 mammoths, which constitute 70% of the animals represented in the cave. These are followed, in order of frequency, by 28 bison, 16 horses, 12 ibexes, 11 rhinoceroses, and a single bear. Thus, only six animal species are represented, but one of them in unusual proportions. Despite the fact that they are next to last in number, the ten rhinoceroses are of some significance, since in other caves they number no more than one or two, except in the Chauvet Cave in Ardèche where there are some 70 of them, albeit dating from a much earlier period.

Few signs are to be found in Rouffignac. Fourteen tectiforms and six serpentiforms – finger-painted wavy lines that resemble (or represent ?) serpents – have been recorded. Other signs include meandering finger-painted shapes that appear throughout the cave and are called macaroni due to their pasta-like shape. These meandering lines cover the equivalent of five hundred square meters on the cave walls, especially on the cavity's ceilings.

Whether it be in black contour paintings or engravings, Rouffignac's is an art form which, in most cases, employs a mastered skill of perfect execution to produce art of exceptional quality.

It is indeed curious that while the Magdalenians probably used the cave quite frequently, they left no material trace of their presence (such as worked flint, butchered animals remains, lamps, etc.). Only a single piece of worked flint was found in the shaft beneath Le Grand Plafond. Nor is their any sign of a living site at the cave's entrance or in the immediate area. Where did the Rouffignac artists come from? As in Lascaux and a number of other decorated caves, Rouffignac evokes the notion of a sanctuary and art used as means to express spiritual or possibly religious thoughts.

The hidden mammoth.
Engravings and paintings were uncovered in Bernifal cave as early as 1902. However, this mammoth was discovered only some 12 years ago. It was hidden in an almost inaccessible corridor, which had not yet been explored. In addition, its style was surprisingly similar to that found in Rouffignac. It was as if the same artist had frequented the two caves.

Due to the lack of archaeological material and any direct dating of pigments, all of which are mineral-based here, the art style was used to date these cave paintings which were probably fairly late Magdalenian images. The great homogeneity of style and technique leads one to believe that a fairly small group of specialists from the same culture – one might even say from the same school – produced works within a set time span.

The cave of one hundred mammoths.
One often reads of "Rouffignac, the cave of one hundred mammoths". In reality, it would be fairer to call it the cave of 158 mammoths. Mammoths represent 70% of the animals featured in the cave. They are drawn in black or engraved on the cave wall. Mammoths appear individually, sometimes in pairs, and often face to face, even in groups of ten, in two opposing herds. Here is the one called "the Patriarch".

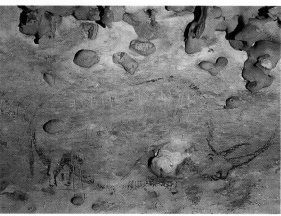

A dangerous herbivore.
Contemporaneous with the mammoth, the woolly rhinoceros is represented ten times in Rouffignac and is depicted in an extraordinary and particularly realistic frieze of three in a row. Very few representations of this animal exist. In the Périgord, however, a few have been found in Lascaux (the scene from the Pit), Les Combarelles, and Font-de-Gaume.

On previous pages:
Le Grand Plafond in Rouffignac.
Near a shaft that leads to a lower galleries of the cave, Le Grand Plafond in Rouffignac was decorated with sixty-three animal drawings. With the exception of the bear, all of the species found in Rouffignac are represented here, including mammoths, bison, horses, ibexes, and rhinoceroses. These animals are not depicted haphazardly. They constitute an organized circular composition in which horses and ibexes are arranged in a particular manner, while the mammoths appear to be more dispersed. This ensemble is even more remarkable when one considers that the floor was originally only 60 centimeters from the ceiling which made it impossible to see the entire composition at one time.

Opposite:
A 15,000 years old portrait of a man (Grotte Saint-Cirq).
Of course, this was not an accurate rendering. None of the prehistoric human representations were exact. Their faces are either caricatures or devoid of detail. This individual was engraved in the rear of the small cave of Saint-Cirq and probably dates to the Middle Magdalenian. The engraving is located in a small depression in the cave's ceiling and is surrounded by several animal figures (ibex, bison, horse), a triangular sign, and two other human profiles. Despite the weak shoulders, the image obviously represents a man. He is sometimes called the sorcerer, but this nickname has no basis whatsoever. Several other animals – horses and bison – are engraved closer to the cave's entrance, and appear to date to Lascaux's period some 17,000 years ago.

A horse from Bara-Bahau (Le Bugue).

The rock which forms the walls and ceiling of this cave is nearly as soft as butter. It is littered with beds of flint in the form of large rounded nodules in the cave walls. Before humans arrived, bears – possibly large cave bears from the Mousterian – frequented this place. They scratched at the walls and left their distinctive claw marks of parallel rows of lines. The engravings, however, are more recent and date to the Magdalenian 15,000 years ago. This horse was engraved using a flint tool. Some lines around the head were made with the fingers. Some lines seem to depict the horses breath leaving its nostrils. The mane is raised as is the case in present-day Asian species. One can also see the hairs of its winter coat visible behind its shoulder. The hoofs were not depicted. A second horse was engraved behind it. Could this be a depiction of a stallion-mare couple?

On following page:
An exceptional site.
In the lower part of its course, the Vézère River makes a series of sinuous curves that meander from one side of the valley to the other. Slightly downriver from Tursac, it forms a near closed loop – or oxbow – before flowing along the cliffs of La Madeleine at the base of which the type site of the Magdalenian is located (left).

Tour 5
From 13,000 to 11,500 years ago (11,000 to 9,500 B.C.) The Upper Magdalenian

With the end of glacial times fast approaching, large Quaternary animals such as the woolly mammoth and rhinoceros, as well as the migrating reindeer, began to disappear. This period was marked by a last bitter resurgence of cold temperatures in the Magdalenian V, followed by another cold but more humid period which gave rise to denser forests in the Magdalenian VI. Reindeer were still present, however deer, roebucks, wild boars, and aurochs appeared or increased in number and constituted the new fauna for the temperate periods to follow.

These last two stages of the Magdalenian are usually defined by the shape of harpoons made from reindeer antlers, whereby the Magdalenian V has unilaterally barbed harpoons and the Magdalenian VI harpoons are bilaterally barbed. However, an occasional harpoon with bilateral barbs may also appear in the first of these two

stages. These objects served as the heads of harpoons. In other words, they were detachable weapons that were fitted onto a wooden haft. An unravelable cord probably enabled the user to recuperate the spear head and the harpooned prey. These objects often have widened bases which may have facilitated the tying of a cord and prevented the piece from slipping. Some more recent harpoons were even perforated for this same purpose.

The last stage of the Magdalenian also saw the emergence of new flint tools, notably parrot-beak burins, points with semi-abrupt lateral retouch (Laugerie-Basse points), some with peduncle (Teyjat points). An increasing number of other forms were also developed that later served as the basis of the Azilian industry. Such implements included Azilian points with curved backs and abrupt retouch, small and short end-scrapers, finely retouched geometrically shaped microliths, and a few flat harpoons from the extreme end of the Magdalenian. The latter were still made from reindeer antler and preceded the Azilian harpoons which were made from red deer antler.

This powerful culture was well represented in the Périgord and left behind works of art, mostly engravings, on cave walls (Teyjat), blocks of stone (Limeuil) and a number of other small objects such as bone, reindeer

Fishing or hunting?
Magdalenian harpoons were generally made from reindeer antler and armed with barbs aligned along the edges. They were probably mounted on hafts which could then be flung using a spear thrower. It is not known whether these weapons were used to fish or hunt (Musée du Périgord).

A masked human.
This bone fragment was discovered in the Magdalenian IV level at the base of the site la Madeleine. It bears an engraving that represents a clearly male human. However, the head is far from human and does not resembles the head of any known animal. It might involve a masked person, like others engraved on pebbles from the same archeological layer (Musée des Eyzies).

In the backdirt of former excavations...
The excavations conducted at la Madeleine, between 1863, the year Lartet and Christy discovered the site, and 1910, when Denis Peyrony intervened on behalf of the State, succeeded in devastating the site. In re-excavating the old backdirt, Peyrony was able to benefit from the "inexperience of the earlier researchers" and salvaged a large limestone slab which bears a splendid carving of a reindeer with a very expressive head (Musée des Antiquités nationales).

antler and stone. The art work ranges from rare artistic quality, sometimes are real miniatures, others are strangely deformed drawings of horses or reindeer with disproportionate heads, and other very schematic or stylized pieces, notably the profiles of female figures.

La Madeleine

The Magdalenian is probably the most prestigious culture of all prehistoric times, particularly in the Reindeer Age, with its abundant reindeer herds.

In the course of their first archaeological exploration in 1863 to 1864, Lartet and Christy were drawn to a vast rock-shelter at the base of a cliff, on the right bank of the Vézère River at the water's edge. The site is unique. In the Tursac plane, the river begins a wide meander which snakes first against the rocky bore of Petit Marzac, then rebounds to the left bank of the valley, and returns to the same bore on the other side. It travels over two kilometers to end less than one hundred meters from its starting point! It flows at the base of the Petit Marzac castle and along the rock-shelter and then snakes away in the direction of Les Eyzies. The excavated area of the site is 50 meters long and 10 to 15 meters wide. Lartet and Christy excavated at least 2.5 meters thick in the central zone. In May 1864, the discovery of a large piece of mammoth tusk generated considerable interest.

This mammoth ivory plaque bears an engraving representing this very same animal. The detail of the engraving demonstrates that it was made by a person who was a contemporary of this animal. The lithic and bone industries from La Madeleine led G. Mortillet to designate this site as the type site for the last period of the Paleolithic. In 1869, he spoke of "the Madeleine Period" and in 1872 he created the term Magdalenian. Oddly enough, despite its notoriety, the site did not suffer too badly from its early attention and did not receive many visitors. Paul Girod, Elie Massénat, and E. Rivière undertook excavations here, but fortunately the antiquities dealer, Otto Hauser, believed La Madeleine to be empty and took no interest in the site. This explains why Denis Peyrony was able to conduct methodical excavations from 1910 until the first World War. This excavation enabled him to distinguish subdivisions in the filling which until then was considered to represent but a single period. The discovery of three, distinct, superposed layers gave rise to a study of the various lithic and bone implements, which defined the types of flint tools, harpoons, or bone points were characteristic of each layer. This information was immediately put to use by Breuil who at the time was defining the major divisions in the Upper Paleolithic. The defined layers at La Madeleine characterized the last three phases of the Magdalenian (IV, V, VI), while the three preceding phases had been defined earlier at Le Placard in Charente.

Before the monograph on the site was published in 1928, Denis Peyrony undertook a small control excavation in 1926, at which point his good fortune led to the discovery of the burial of a child, but from a little more recent period. The site was abandoned for several decades and left to the pillages of clandestine excavators. Fortunately, these untrained excavators returned thousands of times to go through the same backdirt from previous excavations which still contained a wealth of artifacts. Formal excavations were not reopened until 1968 under the direction of Jean-Marc Bouvier. These last excavations defined the stratigraphy and included a number of analyses and carbon 14 dating.

The animal species found at La Madeleine give some indication of the food preferences of the prehistoric populations, but they do not represent all of the existing fauna of the period, in that they correspond only to animals that were hunted and eaten. At La Madeleine, one notes a particular dietary preference for reindeer which, in every layer save one, represent 87-100% of the faunal remains. One layer, Magdalenian IV, contains only 63% reindeer, while horse make up 36% of the remains.

It appears that other species including ibexes, bison, oxen, chamois, and roebucks make up a very small percentage of the Magdalenians' diet. Note that reindeer were not only a source of food, but also provided skins to make tents, bedding, and clothing, as well as bones and antlers to make needles, awls, bone points or harpoons. Their gut and tendons were used as ligatures.

Last but not least, La Madeleine was also an important site for prehistoric art. Hundreds of engraved or sculpted objects originated here. They ranged from the modest to the most spectacular which unfortunately were often removed from the Périgord to national or foreign museums.

Villepin

The site bears the landlord's name and is located a few dozen meters downstream from La Madeleine "in a savory and wild area", writes Peyrony, who discovered the site and excavated it in 1917. Villepin is also a rock-shelter, though partly collapsed, and is well separate from La Madeleine. Two layers were dated to the Magdalenian VI containing bilaterally barbed harpoons which make them contemporaneous with the third phase of La Madeleine's occupation. A third and top layer clearly corresponds to an Azilian occupation for which only a few sporadic traces remain at La Madeleine.

The Magdalenian of Villepin reveals an evolution in the tool assemblage from the lower to the upper layers. This is most evident in the harpoons whose barbs are more pronounced and sharper in the upper layer. The decorations on awls, and bone points are identical to those found in La Madeleine, indicating a certain affinity. The pebbles are engraved with animals which are often difficult to identify, save the horse, of which only the head and withers are portrayed.

A dangerous settlement sheltered by Les Marseilles.

The bottom of this stone cutting dates back to the Middle and Upper Magdalenian. During the Magdalenian IV age, the ceiling collapsed into large, one-meter thick rock slabs. Then other Magdalenian people settled on those slabs and, much later, around 2,700 B.C., Neolithic people did the same thing. More rock slabs collapsed later, thereby forming an impressive chaos.

The spectacular cliffs of Laugerie-Basse.

The site is exceptional. It is located at the base of this high cliff, where one may also find the crystallized cave of Le Grand Roc. Today, the main rock-shelter at Laugerie-Basse, has been gutted of all its archaeological filling, while the Abri des Marseilles (above), located under a clutter of stone rubble 50 meters to the right, was only partially excavated.

Laugerie-Basse

The site is exceptional. It is a huge cliff, over 500 meters long, which overlooks the Vézère River sixty meters away. At its base, and still 15 meters above the valley floor, erosion carved out rock-shelters which were inhabited in various prehistoric periods. Later, the houses of the hamlet of Laugerie-Basse were built into one of these shelters, using the rocky face as the fourth wall and the overhang as part of the roof.

Excavations, initiated in 1863, were conducted under the main rock-shelter, then the site of a farm house, barn, and stable. The laborers, employed by the prehistorians, dug trenches and even tunneled under buildings in a completely disordered fashion. Lartet and Christy and the Marquis Paul de Vibraye and his associate, Franchet, arrived at the site at the same time, followed closely thereafter by Massénat. Attracted by the phenomenal wealth of the site, especially the works of art, many other prehistorians and amateurs soon followed in what became an uninterrupted parade of visitors for the next fifty

The woman and the reindeer, Laugerie-Basse.
Discovered by Abbé Landesque in 1867 or 1868, this work was later purchased by E. Piette who used a lithograph by J. Pilloy in his fine album entitled *L'Art pendant l'âge du renne* (*Art During the Reindeer Age*) which was published in 1907. This strange association between a woman and a reindeer was the subject of much discussion. Despite the absence of breasts, the female nature of the human figure is unmistakable, and the volume of the abdomen suggests that this is a woman in a very advanced stage of pregnancy. It is unfortunate that such an unusual piece was found in such a fragmented state (Musée des Antiquités nationales).

The Chamois Disk.
Perforated bone disks, usually cut from the scapulae of herbivores, have been found in several sites and often date to the Magdalenian IV. This intact disk originated at Laugerie-Basse. Each side bears the portrait of an herbivore, one standing, one resting. Several authors have maintained that they see a chamois on one side associated with a hind on the other (Musée du Périgord).

years. This onslaught of visitors seriously destroyed the integrity of this site, and a number of artifacts, some of them quite impressive, have neither precise stratigraphic nor chronological provenance.

More serious analyses were not carried out until 1912-1913. This research, conducted by Peyrony and Jean Maury only scratched the surface of the classic shelter. A more in-depth excavation was undertaken under the Abri des Marseilles, located 50 meters upstream, which was to be nearly intact at the time. With the patronage of the famous chemist, Joseph-Achille Le Bel, J. Maury was able to dedicate several years to the site's excavation. In 1920, at Le Bel's request, all work was stopped voluntarily, in order to preserve a part of the excavation for future generations. An analysis of the material unearthed at Laugeri-Basse suggests that the site was occupied from the Magdalenian III to the Magdalenian VI and perhaps also briefly in the Azilian. Vestiges of the Neolithic and of the later Bronze Age were also found in the talus outside the shelter's overhang. More is known about the occupation of Abri des Marseilles due to the control section which is still visible. The Magdalenians settled on

The Bison Plaquette of Raymonden.

This rib fragment from a large herbivore is split along its width. A hole was made on the left end to be worn as a pendant. The head of a bison, two isolated limbs, and seven small human silhouettes are featured in a puzzling scene. The barbed line behind the bison's head is also a mystery; it is difficult to interpret it as the animal's vertebral column. One of the human figures carries a forked stick. This type of association between a bison and stylized humans is also found on another engraved bone from the site of Château des Eyzies which also dates to the Upper Magdalenian (Musée du Périgord).

Fluttering Birds of Raymonden.

These small birds seem to have been captured in mid-flight, between two ibexes travelling in single file (seen in the opposite direction). One can discern another ibex and two other heads of young animals, possibly ibexes or bovines (Musée du Périgord).

the shelter's natural floor 14,000 years ago. This occupation lasted until the Magdalenian VI, when a large section of the overhang suddenly collapsed. Large and thick limestone blocks covered a section of the living site. Nevertheless, the Magdalenians returned and left a few signs of their occupation atop the fallen boulders. The shelter was then abandoned for a long time.

Around 2,000 B.C., Neolithic people arrived from the Artenac culture. A layer of ash and charcoal were dated to this period, which covered the entire excavated surface of the rock-shelter. The distribution of this combustion debris over such a vast space still cannot be explained. This occupation was followed by further disintegration of the cliff face which left an impressive pile of boulders eight to ten meters high.

Laugerie-Basse's acclaim stems essentially from its wealth in Magdalenian art. The "immodest Venus", "the Woman and the Reindeer", and many others are quite famous. All of these pieces are now dispersed across the globe, many of them at the Musée des Antiquités Nationales, the Musée de l'Homme and the British Museum.

Raymonden

Our Magdalenian itinerary now leaves the Vézère Valley to travel further north to the Isle valley and its small tributary, the Beauronne. Four or five kilometers from Périgueux, slightly upstream from Chancelade and its Romanic monastery, an eight hundred meter stretch of cliffs was intensively quarried for cut stone. The small prehistoric cave-site of Raymonden is located by the side of the road, between two rock quarries. Several centuries ago, at this site, an embankment of limestone at cave level was quarried and used to build the grinding stones of mill. Some vestiges of this activity are still visible. The prehistoric site was discovered in March 1876 by M. Hardy, then a correspondent for the Ministère de l'instruction publique, and future archivist and conservator for the Musée du Périgord.

He excavated Raymonden for a while and was succeeded in 1883 by two High School teachers. The site was then left idle until 1887, when the Department built a small railroad line from Périgueux to Brantôme. Ballast was needed, and the talus of Raymonden fit the bill. Laborers

A Strange Animal in Rochereil.
One would be hard pressed to identify the species of this long necked animal with a strange head portrayed above a small engraved motif. Could it be an awkwardly drawn tufted bird or an imaginary animal? (Musée de Brantôme)

Perforated and Decorated Baton.
Located close to Rochereil, La Peyzie has yielded several decorated objects from the Upper Magdalenian. This perforated baton, made from reindeer antler, bears a puzzling engraved pattern. Could it be a plant motif? (private collection, copy at Musée de Brantôme)

dug into the archaeological strata and spread bone and worked flint along nearly three kilometers of tracks, we are told. When the extent of the damage was realized, M. Hardy and M. Féaux decided to conduct a methodical excavation lasting from October 1887 to October 1888. The high point of the dig was a rare discovery of a human burial. In his monograph, published in 1891, Hardy divided the 1.35 meter-thick "archaeological layer" into four "living floors", each separated by thin layers of sandy or clay soils, which was quite praiseworthy work for this period. The worked bone or flint, faunal remains, and works of art from this site are now preserved at the Musée du Périgord. Unfortunately, no record was made of the provenance of these objects within the caves stratified deposits. Therefore we have lost invaluable information on the chronological origin of these artifacts. The most we can say, given the presence of certain distinctive materials, is that the entire collection corresponds to the period from Magdalenian IV to VI. The most famous work of art is the "bison plaquette" whose subject is comparable to another plaquette from the same period in Les Eyzies. This plaquette has been the subject of a number of descriptions and interpretations, some of which are quite picturesque and whimsical. The burial was found at the base of the site. The body had been laid on its left side, in a tightly flexed position, with the left hand under the head and the right hand under the chin. As was often the case in the Upper Paleolithic, the body had been sprinkled with iron oxide which gave the bones a reddish tint.

Anatomist Léo Testut studied the remains and determined that they constituted a particular fossil type or *Homo sapiens* race that differed from Cro-Magnon and

Grimaldi: the Chancelade race. This race was rather small (approximately 1.6 meter tall), with elongated crania, high and flat foreheads, and high, broad faces. Chancelade hominids were once compared to the Inuits of Labrador and Greenland whose tool assemblages and lifestyles in similar climatic conditions were somewhat analogous. Today, such comparisons and associations are no longer considered valid, and even the notion of "race" has been dropped. Instead, irregularities in the fossil record of *Homo sapiens* are attributed to individual variation, sexual dimorphism or discrete evolutionary diversity.

In 1927, Louis Didon, a hotel manager in Périgueux and an amateur prehistorian, undertook excavations prior to and immediately after the excavations of Féaux and Hardy. Following his death, J. Bouyssonie succeeded him from 1928 to 1929. The four layers excavated corresponded to the first three stages of the Magdalenian. Thus, had earlier excavations preserved the upper layers, Raymonden would have been the sole site in which a study of the six continuous cultural deposits from the Magdalenian might have been possible. The site itself was excavated too early. But then, might the same not be said for sites currently being excavated?

Rochereil

We now move on to the Dronne Valley, upstream from the small town of Lisle. The site is adjacent to the Rochereil mill, in a small ten meter square cavity and extends onto a larger terrace in front. Féaux and the Marquis de Fayolle conducted the first excavation here at the turn of the 20th century – an excavation which almost cost the life of one of them in a rock fall. However from 1935 to 1939, the best excavations were carried out by

Teyjat

The Bandiat valley, in which Teyjat is located, is not confined to the Périgord region. The valley passes through parts of Abjat, on the border of the Departments of the Dordogne and Haute-Vienne; it then drops into Nontron and climbs northwest to enter the Charente. Its path outlines almost the entire area of the granitic block which occupies a small region of the Department's northern territory. At Teyjat, the Bandiat Valley is still in limestone country, a zone highly valued by Paleolithic peoples for its rock-shelters and caves.

The grotte de la Mairie is on the outskirts of the village, near the grade school and the municipal office. Two caves split off from a common entrance. The small gallery is forty meters long, while the long gallery, which is of interest here, is some seventy-five meters long, though the Magdalenian zone does not extend farther than the first fifteen meters. The prehistoric entrance to the site was discovered in 1889 by Perrier du Carne, and though his published study on Teyjat was subtitled "Magdalenian engravings", it was based on the engravings he found on bones and not the parietal engravings discovered in 1903. Perrier du Carne's excavation of the site was somewhat limited but productive. In addition to barbed harpoons, he found five art objects, including one representation of a pony-like horse, engraved on an unusual medium – a reindeer sacrum.

Perrier du Carne made one observation that is very disturbing. He stated that within a block of dirt removed with a blow from a pick, he found an imprint in the form of a 1.35 meter-long bow which was still filled with the remains of decomposed wood. Its form was fairly comparable to the well-preserved bows of the Danish Mesolithic. If the bow at la Mairie is indeed from the Magdalenian, it remains the only evidence of its use in this period.

In 1903, on the advice of H. Breuil and Emile Cartailhac, Denis Peyrony too travelled to Teyjat to see whether the cave contained engravings like those he had found in the Les Eyzies region. Indeed, it did. The engravings were made on a calcite film which covered stalagmite formations. Some were in place, others were on fragmented blocks.

Dr P.-E. Jude who went on to publish his findings in 1960.

Two cultural assemblages were identified in the stratigraphy and each was subdivided into several levels. One belongs to the Magdalenian VI well defined by its lithic and bone industry including numerous parrot-beak burins, Laugerie-Basse points, Teyjat points, bilaterally barbed harpoons, and works of art in a style typical of this phase in the Magdalenian. The second assemblage was Azilian and contained a rich assemblage of points typical of this period along with flat harpoons made from deer antler. One human burial and the burnt remains of two adolescents were also unearthed and belong to a period we explore further on.

The excavations conducted in 1904 by Paul Bourrinet, a grade school teacher in Teyjat, led to new discoveries and a detailed study of the living site which extended about fifteen meters from entrance into the cave. Bourrinet's detailed observations, under the supervision of Peyrony and Breuil, revealed two distinct layers separated by a sterile layer of rubble. The oldest layer dates to the Magdalenian V which is characterized by unilaterally barbed harpoons. The upper layer is from the Magdalenian VI with bilaterally barbed harpoons, parrot-beak burins, and stemmed flint points, later known as Teyjat points.

Several portable art objects were also unearthed at this site. One very surprising piece was an eagle radius upon which a herd of reindeer was portrayed. The first three heads were complete, the thirteen or fourteen that followed were represented by their antlers and oblique hatched lines formed a continuous band at the body level. The head of the last reindeer to close the ranks is also complete.

The surfaces of the limestone walls in the cave are not suitable for engraving. The Magdalenians therefore made use of formations of amber calcite to engrave their images. Parts of the calcite were fractured by falling rubble, and today the engravings are found on slabs of stone, some lying flat, others resting vertically in the archaeological matrix of the Magdalenian V. So it is possible that these engravings date to this first period of occupation. This is one of the rare cases in which parie-

A photographic realism.

The end of the Magdalenian is marked by a drawing style with a photograph-like realism. This engraving of a cow at Teyjat illustrates the very realistic proportions and posture. It is immediately followed by an aurochs male whose snout is visible here.

tal art can be dated directly, since it was found in an archaeological layer.

These engravings form two distinct groups. All the images of the group furthest from the entrance can be clustered together. They form a semi-circular composition which begins at the base with a horse turned to the right, above which three aurochs – one male between two females – walk to the left. Higher still near the top of the calcite, a succession of red deer, reindeer, horses, two bison, and a bear are depicted facing in different directions. The images of a second group are more difficult to cluster. This group also associates red deer, a reposed reindeer, a fawn, horses, and a bear.

Forty-eight animals in all were counted at Teyjat including 5 unidentified deer species, 11 red deer, 13 reindeer, 10 horses, 3 aurochs, 4 bison, and 2 bears. Deer represent two-thirds of the fauna portrayed which is an unusual proportion in cave art where horses (Lascaux and Les Combarelles), bison (Font-de-Gaume), and on rare occasions mammoths (Rouffignac and Bernifal) generally dominate. The number of reindeer (over a quarter of the images) is also unusually high.

The end of the reindeer age.
At Limeuil, reindeer were the most frequently represented animals, whereas previously they were either relatively scarce in number on the walls of caves (Font-de-Gaume and Les Combarelles) or absent (Rouffignac) (Musée du Périgord).

The last hunters of the Vézère.
At Limeuil, the Vézère flows into the Dordogne. This was once the living site of the last great hunters of the reindeer age. The Magdalenian site is now covered by the houses of a medieval village. More than a hundred slabs, plaques and plaquettes were uncovered bearing the engraved images of reindeer, horses, red deer, ibexes, aurochs, and bears. Some believe that Limeuil was once the site of a veritable "atelier".

The finely incised engravings are of a particular style characterized by a photograph-like realism in the animal's general behavior, proportions, and details. Along with the slightly more recent engravings at Limeuil, they help define the standards of an artistic style – the recent style IV according to A. Leroi-Gourhan – which marks the end of the Magdalenian.

Limeuil

No visible trace of Limeuil's prehistoric occupation remains, because the site, which was excavated at the start of the 20th century, extends beneath the houses, gardens, and narrow streets of the small village, in front of a limestone outcrop which overlooks the confluence of the Vézère and Dordogne Rivers. Credit for the discovery of the site goes to a retired colonial doctor who uncovered the site, while ground work was being conducted at the home of the village baker, Léo Bélanger. The excavation was conducted from 1909 to 1913 by prehistorian J. Bouyssonie from Brive, who was mandated and financed by la Direction des Beaux-Arts. The excavation was quite arduous and had to proceed using test pits, trenches, and underground tunnels to follow the

This horse is characteristic of Limeuil engravings which date to the Magdalenian VI. This drawing has an almost academic realism which is very different from Lascaux, five thousand years earlier (Musée des Antiquités nationales).

archaeological strata, in order to respect the structures overhead.

The excavated site extended for a thirty meters along the base of a slope below two outcrops of limestone and constituted an open air site with the use of a small cliff overhang upslope. The strata date to the Magdalenian VI and are characterized by an overabundance of parrot-beak burins and bilaterally barbed harpoons. The engravings on bone and reindeer antler are characteristic of the period. Other objects included a beautiful perforated baton decorated with fishes and macrocephalic reindeer, and other pieces featuring bison, horses and even a fox, a species rarely depicted in prehistoric art.

The novelty of this site of Limeuil is the abundance of engraved limestone plaquettes, plaques and blocks. Bouyssonie published descriptions of over a hundred objects. Limeuil was seen by him as the site of a prehistoric art workshop, and he compared its art objects to the pages of a sketchbook. Some are rough sketches which are often jumbled together, others works are more detailed, and still others are true master pieces.

This very romantic explanation does not stem from a very rigorous scientific analysis which might otherwise eliminate some of its more imaginative aspects. However, it would be difficult to replace this interpretation with another that could explain a site so rich in engraved stones of all sizes which seem to have been discarded along side flaked flint tools and food remains. It is difficult to imagine Limeuil as a sanctuary composed of portable art.

What is certain is that these pieces are of a rare quality and display a marked stylistic homogeneity. As in Teyjat, we find representations with photograph-like rea-

Headless women.

The last Magdalenians, who drew very realistic animals, sometimes also made very simplified female profiles which consisted of torsos and backsides without heads, arms, or legs. Several Lalinde blocks could not be placed stratigraphically until the discovery of another block bearing this female representation under the nearby rock-shelter of Gare de Couze. Observations made by Professor Bordes, who excavated the site, allowed for exact dates to be attributed to these objects which are Magdalenian VI in age (Musée des Eyzies).

lism in anatomical details, proportions, and behavior: a lowered head of a grazing reindeer, rutting reindeer, a herd of red deer in which one has its head raised on the alert, galloping horses, etc. On several occasions, a line drawn at the animals' feet seems to indicate the ground level which is rarely depicted in Paleolithic art. And like Teyjat, red deer and reindeer are the most common and constitute half of the animals represented, followed by horses (a third), oxen, bison, and ibexes. Two bears were also present.

Thus it is here, where the Vézère flows into the Dordogne, that we come to the end of this prestigious tour of the Magdalenian. This royal tour of prehistory took us from Lascaux to Limeuil, and in a distance of thirty kilometers, covered more than five thousand years time.

DATES (B.C.)	PERIOD
	Late Iron Age
	Early Iron Age
-1000	Late Bronze Age
	Middle Bronze Age
-2000	Early Bronze Age
	Late Neolithic
-3000	Later Neolithic
-4000	Middle Neolithic
-5000	Early Neolithic
-6000	
-7000	Mesolithic
-8000	
-9000	

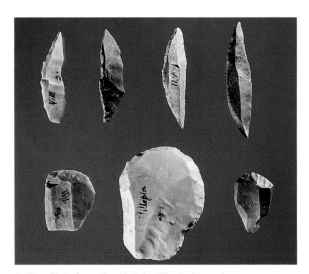

Azilian flints from the Abri de Villepin (Tursac).

The Azilian flint points, identical to points from the later Magdalenian, were used as projectile. Other tools like the short endscraper, truncated blade, and the burin could be used in everyday activities to work hides and bone, and cut wood (private coll.).

From 9,500 to 3,000 B.C. Towards the Mesolithic and Neolithic

Around 9,500-9,000 B.C., due to a relatively temperate oscillation, the reindeer began to leave the Périgord which no longer provided its usual food source – lichen. The landscape had ceased to be the steppe with sparse tree cover that was once the home of Magdalenian hunters. Humidity favored the growth of deciduous trees. The previously open land darkened and so did men's life in Périgord. Their world was disintegrating. Their favorite game became scarce, and rain flooded their camps. One last rigorous cold period hinted that the good times would return, but alas, the glacial times were gone forever. The reindeer would no longer return nor would the many animals frequently featured in cave paintings. The time of forest animals had arrived. These included red deer, boar, roe deer, and less remarkable small game, more difficult to hunt because they did not live in large herds but rather alone or in small groups. The traditional hunts and the good times were no more!

The last reindeer were hunted 11 to 12,000 years ago in the Dordogne valley at Couze and round the Morin rock-shelter near Pessac-sur-Dordogne (today located in Gironde, near its border with the Périgord). Did they first retreat to the cooler regions of the Pyrenees or the Massif Central in the warm summer months like the ibex? Were they able to travel north and reach the latitudes at which reindeer live today? Whatsoever, contrary to an all too popular belief, the Magdalenians did not follow the reindeer to northern regions. Their direct offsprings, the Azilians, stayed in the country where their abilities to adapt were put to the test, until a new lifestyle could develop.

The Azilian toolkit clearly derives from the preceding period. The relatively minor changes consist of shorter, more numerous end-scrapers, burins are less numerous, and less diverse too. However, the great tradition of tools made from reindeer antler was lost with the disappearance of the reindeer.

Were these the effects of a more precarious lifestyle? The caves and rock-shelters no longer seem to attract the prehistoric painters or engravers. Azilian artists preferred to paint or engrave stone or bone plaquettes, and pebbles, as if they avoided consecrating permanent sanctuaries. These were the last expressions of a naturalist art. The engravings of horses or bovids displayed a very different style from the Magdalenian, even from the preceding Magdalenian VI. However, when we examine the series of lines engraved on limestone pebbles, like the one from Rochereil, we can no longer decipher the message Azilian artists tried to transmit, unless they knowingly and deliberately hid this message in their graphic designs.

The heirs of reindeer hunters, who learned to hunt deer and boar, were fortunate that fishing was an option, since the aquatic life was less directly affected by the climatic changes. As for the Magdalenians before them, some Azilian campsites, like Rochereil and Pont d'Ambon, or La Madeleine and Villepin were located at the edge of the Dronne and Vézère Rivers respectively. The abundance of fish at Pont d'Ambon practically makes it a specialized site. The reoccupation of the previous Magdalenian sites is a sign of continuity even though temporary open air camps were established elsewhere.

The only known skeletal remains of Périgord Azilians are those of a medium sized male (1.6 meters high) from Rochereil with some characteristics similar to the "Chancelade race", and two individuals – one male, one female – from Peyrat at Saint-Rabier near Terrasson. In the latter case, the male was 1.67 meters high and the female only 1.56 meters. The man's face was rather broad. The woman's skull was missing.

A strange horse.
This engraving belongs to the Azilian period at Pont d'Ambon and is one of the rare figurative engravings known from this period. Its style is original and unrelated to that of the Magdalenian. The head and legs are filled with hatched lines and the outline is accented by tiny criss-crosses and extremely fine incisions. The animal's proportions are surprising. The body is abnormally long and the legs are dwarfed (Musée des Eyzies).

Azilian harpoon with a perforated base from Rochereil.
The flat Azilian harpoons are not as impressive as the Magdalenian harpoons, but the spongy nature of the material did not allow for anything better. It is questionable as to whether harpoons were used for fishing. They may have been used for hunting or even suspended as hooks (Musée de Brantôme).

Mesolithic settlement in the porch of Rouffignac cave.
Between 9,200-7,800 years ago, Mesolithic hunters settled the porch area of Rouffignac cave. Stratified hearths, animal bones, and worked flakes – especially geometric microliths from the Sauveterrian – were uncovered. The upper levels held burials from the Neolithic and the Age of Metals.

Campniac cave, Coulounieix-Chamiers.
Campniac cave is located in the small valley of Vieille-Cité near Périgueux. It yielded partially cremated human bones, polished stone axes, flaked flints, bone tools, and ornaments. The human remains probably belong to people who lived on the Ecornebœuf hillside overlooking the valley.

The Mesolithic and Early Neolithic: from the woods to open clearings
The Mesolithic culture: forest hunters

The climate was still dry and cold, but not glacial, and conditions gradually became milder over time. Pine and birch progressively declined. Then hazel and oak forests began to obscure the Périgord's horizon. Gradually, a large pristine forest started growing, inhabited by game animals, fur-bearers, and dangerous carnivores like bears and wolves.

Humans developed the bow and arrow for survival and self-defense. The bow, one of the first man-made machines, may have originated in the Upper Paleolithic, but post-glacial hunters, the forest dwellers, adopted it as their prefered weapon. The bows of Northern Europe, made of yew wood, give some idea of the lost bows of the Périgord's Mesolithic. The arrow is a precision weapon, superior to the spear, and very deadly with speeds exceeding one hundred kilometers per hour. Prehistoric hunters armed their arrows with miniature flint points. The smallest points were only a few millimeters long and weighed less than one gram. They were probably mounted on reed stalks using resin, or fish or other animal glues. Sometimes traces of these adhesives can still be discerned on these tiny worked flints, or microliths, micropoints or geometrics: triangles, segments or trapezes.

Hunters' life was not a sedentary one. They moved

The engraved pebble of Rochereil.
This small six centimeter long limestone pebble, coated with ochre, is decorated on one side with fine regular incisions organized into ten separate sections. What could be the meaning hidden behind these complex motifs? Magic? Sorcery?

Polishing stone from Carves. Flaked axes were polished by rubbing them on blocks of siliceous sandstone using a mixture of an abrasive (e.g. sand) and a binding agent. This could take ten hours or more. The deep grooves have been used for the cutting edge of the axes. The shallower oval grooves served for the blades and flanges (Musée du Périgord).

round their hunting and fishing territories, fully exploited seasonal resources, and collected fruits, seeds, and wildberries along the way like all forest dwellers. Open air camps are still largely unknown in the Périgord. The selected places were rock-shelters or cave porchs like Contie cave at Coulaures in the Isle basin, and especially Rouffignac cave in the Vézère basin. For over a thousand years, hunters returned here to camp, knap flint (whose nodules were at hand in the calcareous cave walls), and light fires surrounded by stakes maybe used to hold spits to roast the boar or red deer hunted in the area.

They left tiny flints characteristic of the Sauveterrian culture which name is derived from the type-site Sauveterre-la-Lémance, located in the historic (although not administrative) Périgord. Microliths, pygmy triangles, sharpened bipoints (Sauveterrian points), points with truncated bases (Rouffignac points), were made in situ, since we find microburins and flint knapping debitage associated with them. Larger tools such as end-scrapers, and especially denticulates, could have been used for other activities like working wood. Some flint knives show a special gloss as if the had cut silicious stems. However, it is unlikely that these plants were cereal stalks, since wild cereals existed only in the Near East, and cereal culture did not appear in the West until later in the Neolithic. The inhabitants of Rouffignac probably harvested plants for litter or basketry.

Had the dog already been domesticated? It is quite possible. Immediately after glacial times, small wolves could be either in the process of domestication or already domesticated. They may be the ancestors to our dogs.

Middle Neolithic vessel from Campniac cave.
Campniac was occupied during the Middle, Late and Later Neolithic. This round bottomed pot is Middle Neolithic, as well as several transverse arrowheads, polished axes, and ornaments from this cave (Musée du Périgord).

Laugerie-Haute, the Abri du Squelette.

This rock-shelter yielded at least three skeletons casually found in 1938, when large fallen blocks were destroyed. The bones belong to a man over 60, and another, 25 to 30 years old. The third could not be examined. Some characteristics, as an elongated skull, a fairly wide face and nose, and low orbits, seem to link them to Upper Paleolithic or Mesolithic populations. An Early-Middle Neolithic pot was discovered in close vicinity.

In any case, dogs did accompany the last Mesolithic inhabitants of Rouffignac 8,000 years ago.

It is unclear what Périgord Mesolithic peoples looked like.

The first step towards a farming culture
7,000 years ago, several significant changes occurred which had happened long before in the eastern part of the Mediterranean basin. A new lifestyle gradually changed the hunters of the forest into the first agriculturalists. What prompted this first spark? What made these last hunters become the first farmers and shepherds? The first signs appear a thousand years earlier with a change in the toolkit. Gradually, trapezes replace the triangles, and microliths become larger. True transverse arrowheads, generally triangular with invasive retouch, appear at Rouffignac, Roc du Barbeau, and Peyrat near Saint-Rabier. At Rouffignac, the level dates from the middle of the 6th millennium, after carbon 14 dating. These tiny

arrowheads and the first associated microliths with invasive retouch are found throughout Southern France. They belonged to the first shepherds and farmers of the Neolithic.

The Stone Axe farmers
The Polished Stone culture
The new dawn for humanity was marked by the emergence of a rural economy based on animal husbandry and plant cultivation. Efficient tools were needed to cut down trees, make clearings in the forest, turn up the fertile top soil, sow precious seeds, protect the crops from trampling, and harvest and store the grains. In the beginning, Neolithic farmers continued to use the tools inherited from their Mesolithic predecessors, but they soon invented new ones. For the heavy work like cutting trees and breaking the top soil, as well as other more delicate tasks, the polished axe became the basic Neolithic tool. Rich in flint and hard cobblestones, the Périgord was

The Blanc chambered tomb at Beaumont or Cros-de-la-Vuige.
This megalith, often incorrectly called "the gallery grave of Blanc at Beaumont", is located on a natural mound probably heavily altered by Neolithic people. Its present state does not reflect the original architecture. An additional kerbstone was added along the length of the chamber. Today one enters from the back of the megalith, while the original entrance was at the opposite end through a now collapsed portal, characteristic of the Anjou type monuments.

an excellent source of raw materials. The grey-greenish dolerite pebbles carried by the Auvézère from the Limousin, were rolled by the Isle River to be deposited just downstream from Périgueux. There, they were ultimately transformed into polished (or ground) stone axes. In the East of the *département*, however, around Saint-Jean-de-Côle, quarries have recently been discovered. The excellent flint deposits round Bergerac supplied an axe production workshops.

Middle Neolithic burials in caves and megaliths
When these workshops appeared, approximately 5,000 years ago, farming and animal breeding communities were already settled in the Périgord region. Their villages, still not well known, could have been seated on rocky spurs where the natural erosion and thousands years of agriculture have erased any trace. Others settled lower in the valleys and are possibly buried in the alluvial deposits. Among the rock-shelters or caves occupied

The Point-du-Jour megalith (Vergt-de-Biron).
At the border between the Dordogne and Lot-et-Garonne, the Point-du-Jour megalith rises on a promontory overlooking the Dropt Valley. Its enormous, six meters long, grey sandstone capstone rests upon two rows of kerbstones which collapsed under its weight. This is definitely not a passage grave, but it may be an Anjou type chambered tomb, like the Blanc one, whose entrance structures should be destroyed.

during that period, the Neolithic deposits were often destroyed by earlier excavators in search of Paleolithic remains, like in the famous sites of Les Eyzies, such as Laugerie-Basse, Laugerie-Haute, La Mouthe, among others.

The megaliths: house of the dead or monument for the living?

From the middle of the 5th millenium onwards, strange monuments made of slabs of raw or coarsely worked stone called megaliths appeared in the Périgord and in nearby Charente. Erect stone slabs delineate polygonal or rectangular chambers which are covered by a large cap-stone. This chamber is preceded by a passage made of shorter vertical stone slabs or dry-stone wallings covered by capstones. Perhaps, as in neighbouring Charente, the Périgord saw the emergence of megaliths entirely built of dry-stone masonry with corbel chambers like the "bories" of our ancestors. These constructions were usually covered by rubble supported by dry-stone wallings or by earthen mounds (burial mounds). Once buried under their mound, the monuments looked like caves. Unfortunately, time and human activity have altered these monuments. Deprived of their mound and their passage, and reduced to a few leaning or collapsed slabs, they are now no more than pathetic ruins.

A pot from the Campniac cave.
A flat-based vessel with lugs. Coarse clay with vegetal temper, awkward modelling, and low temperature firing were all characteristics of Late Neolithic (Musée du Périgord).

Campniac ornaments.
This necklace is a modern assemblage of dispersed finds from the cave, including drilled animal teeth, stone beads and a limestone pendant (Musée du Périgord).

Boat-shaped battle-axe from Saint-Sulpice de Mareuil.
This boat-shaped axe is made of imported stone (hornblendite possibly from Brittany). Similar axes have been found in the Val de Loire. Given their elaborate shape and the softness of the rock from which they are made, they probably had a more symbolic than utilitarian value (private collection).

The number of megaliths in the Périgord is still largely underestimated. The one hundred registred monuments is a respected figure for a French region, but nearly everything was robbed by treasure hunters who were surely left disappointed. Thus, we often have no idea as to what they once contained, their date of construction, nor their original architecture. They must have been is use for a millenium at least, but it is only by comparing them with others in the neighbouring regions, especially Southwest France, that it is possible to situate them chronologically.

Settlements and collective burials in caves
during the Later Neolithic
As the last megaliths were being erected, the Périgord's landscape was changing. In the beginning of the 4th millennium B.C., cultures from the Charente, Matignons, and Peu-Richard, of the Late Neolithic radiated outward to the basins of the Dronne and the Isle rivers. Compared to the Middle Neolithic ware, their pottery was of equal quality. They made some fine pots with incised or relief decoration. Flaked or polished stone tools were far more abundant. Other new implements include axe-hammers, double-axes, and polished perforated spherical maceheads. Their making was time-consuming and difficult, and the end product was fragile. They were probably not tools but rather insignias of some high authority. Their symbolic power might have been comparable to the double-axe of Aegean civilization. To this day, about thirty such axes or fragments have been found in the Périgord.

Like their neighbours in Charente, the inhabitants of the Dordogne adopted or developed causewayed camps. On high grounds or even on the plains, interrupted ditches were dug out, forming more or less circular enclosures, either single or multiple. Aerial photograph revealed a few of these in the north of Périgord. Excavations in Bouteilles-Saint-Sébastien and Festalemps evidenced traces of the Matignon culture, dating from the Late Stone Age. These ditches, dug with antler or flint picks, could also have been quarries. The extracted raw materials were used to build up banks, walls, and perhaps smaller constructions, such as dwellings and annexes, completely destroyed since by erosion and centuries of plowing. It is unclear why people dug series of interrupted ditches in sandy soils as in the Isle valley (Fontaine de la Demoiselle at Saint-Léon-sur-l'Isle).

More is known about the burials of this period than about the settlements. Collective burials, sometimes with several dozen skeletons, were discovered in caves in the Isle basin at Campniac or in the Dordogne basin at Eybral. Often the bones had been removed, reordered and even

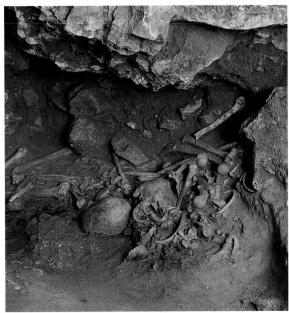

An overview of Eybral cave at Le Coux-et-Bigaroque.
Opened in the small valley of a tributary of the Dordogne River, it was practically filled with clay and contained a jumble of bones from nearly eighty-five skeletons of men, women, and children, some of them burnt. This collective burial dates back to the Late Neolithic (now on display in the Musée d'Aquitaine).

Trepanated skull, Eybral cave.
The skull of a young adult with two healed trepanations, one very large (90 mm long by 55 mm wide) on the top, the other on the rear part (50 mm by 40 mm). There is no sign of infection, which demonstrates the effectiveness of the surgeons who operated using flint tools (Musée d'Aquitaine).

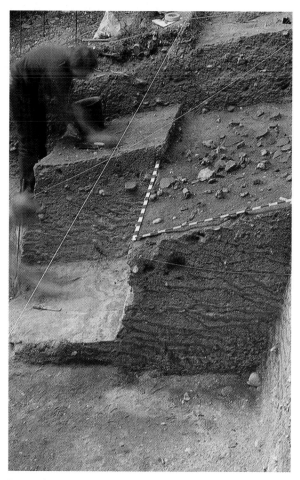

Excavation at Fontaine de la Demoiselle, Saint-Léon-sur-l'Isle (excavation by J. Roussot-Larroque).
This site was occupied in the Late Neolithic (striated bands in the whitish sand) and then in the Later Neolithic (reddish brown sand). A ditch dug into the sands by the first settlers were re-excavated by the Artenacians of the Later Neolithic.

A large building dating from the Later Stone Age in Douchapt – ground plan and hypothetical reconstruction.
Two vast oblong constructions dating from the Later Stone Age (Artenacian culture) were discovered on the bank of the River Dronne by the traces left in the soil. After the hypothetical reconstruction, a line of huge wooden posts supported a ridge piece and the edges of the roof rested on smaller peripheral posts. The walls were built of daub. Each building covered a ground area of more than 1,000 sq. meters and each was flanked by a fenced enclosure.

Baked clay figurine from Les Plaguettes at Razac-de-Saussignac.
From a site occupied by the Artenacians, this mask figurine is six centimeters long. Its features are anthropomorphic, with a flat nose, lips projecting outward, and a pointed chin. Today, this very expressive and strange figurine is the only one of its kind from French Neolithic art (private collection).

sometimes cremated. The grave goods were often poor and included a rare polished axe (usually made of flint), coarse flat-based pottery, perforated animal teeth, limestone beads, disks with two holes made from bone or the mother of pearl from fresh water mussels. The cultural assemblage, associated with these tombs, has come to be called "the Isle-Dordogne group". The same population may have reused or even built their own dolmens. The gallery graves in the southern Périgord (Marsalès) may date to this period, but they have long since been robbed of all their contents. Based on several traits in the funerary ritual and the implements associated with the burials, this Isle-Dordogne group of the Périgord seems to closely resemble the Seine-Oise-Marne group from the Late Neolithic in the Paris basin.

Thanks to these large series of bones, information have been gained about the skeletal morphology of the Péri-

Flint "dagger" from Saint-Seurin-de-Prats.
The dorsal face bears regular oblique retouch, made after the piece was polished. These "daggers" were used for peaceful purposes. The most perfectly flaked were prestige items. Some of them – as this one – were made using imported flint blades from the Grand Pressigny workshops, near Tours (private collection).

Flint "dagger" from the Périgord.
The two parts of this long blade from Chancelade were uncovered eleven years apart. It is over 23 centimeters long and retouched along the edges and at the point. This blade illustrates the knapping techniques of the Later Neolithic.

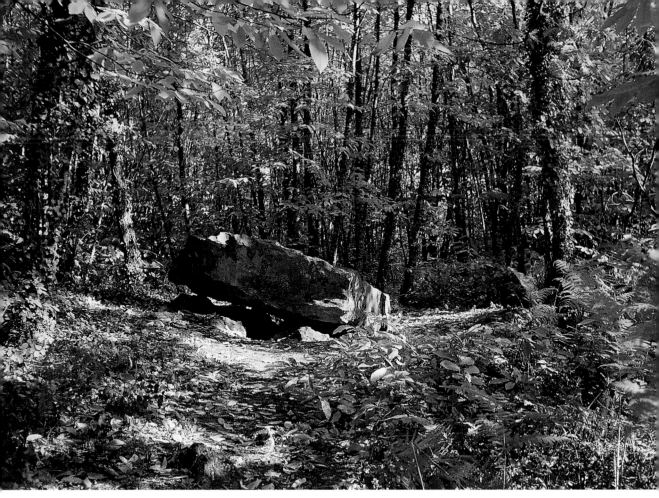

The Bonarme megalith in Saint-Pardoux-et-Vielvic.

The megalith de Cayrelea, or "Lou Ped de la Vache", is still half buried within an earthen mound and covered with earth. The present entrance into the trapezoidal chamber is between the back stone and one of the kerbstones. The capstone is supported by two large parallel blocks forming a passage. This capstone bears two natural depressions which common people see as a cow's hoofprints.

gord populations of about 4,700 years before. In many ways, they resemble their ancestors. It is unlikely that immigrations changed the fundamental characteristics of this population. Their skulls were elongated, sometimes carinated, and their faces were fairly wide, but they were probably generally less robust than Upper Paleolithic populations. Changes in living conditions may account for a great deal. The selection pressures which were still quite high in the Upper Paleolithic decreased gradually in the Neolithic. A drop in the meat content of the diet and increased protection against the elements and other dangers, also meant a far more favorable environment for the sick, the elderly, and children. The ensuing gracilization is clearly visible. This process is equivalent to skeletal reductions observed in domesticated animals compared to their wild ancestors. Humans are self-domesticated animals.

"Livres de beurre" of Lamonzie-Montastruc. These Bergerac flint cores were prepared for the pressure debitage of long blades, using the special technique of the Grand Pressigny workshops (private collection).

Changes during the Later Neolithic
The appearance of the first copper objects towards the end of the third millenium did not spell the immediate disappearance of the Neolithic civilization. Perhaps stimulated by competition with the new metal, flint knapping reached new heights with winged arrowheads and

The megalith at Cantegrel in Saint-Chamassy.
Partly buried beneath a bank, the Cantegrel megalith has a rectangular chamber. One of the kerbstones shows grooved marks from its use as a polishing stone. An excavation during the late 19th century reportedly uncovered a skeleton lying diagonally in this chamber and holding a flint implement in its hand.

large retouched blades, or "daggers", at times more than 20 centimeters long. Flint blades were imported from Grand Pressigny near Tours, knapped from specially prepared cores called "pounds of butter" (livres de beurre). Flint knappers from the Bergerac region tried in vain to equal them. "Livres de beurre" have been found near Lanquais and in the Montclar forest.

The Périgord was then in the realm of a very dynamic culture, the Artenacian, extending from Normandy to Limousin and Quercy. Fine ceramics had incised or pointillé decoration. The typical handles were beak or nose shaped. The settlements are found on highlands, on the slope of plateaux, in valleys, and even at the water's edge. Cultivators and animal breeders, the Artenacians even colonized sandy soils until then sparsely populated. They settled in the Dronne, Isle, Vézère, and Dordogne basins. Great earthmovers, the Artenacians dug ditches, built earthen and stone ramparts, and planted wooden posts in marshlands. In Douchapt in the Dronne Valley,

recent excavations revealed the plans of two large houses. They probably had daub walls and a roof made of thatch or reeds.

Caves, rock-shelters and megaliths could be used for collective burials. They reused megaliths and perhaps built new ones. Often smaller and simpler than in the Middle Neolithic, they were quite numerous particularly in the Isle basin (Saint-Aquilin) and in southern Périgord (Saint-Pardoux-et-Vielvic).

From 3,500 to 850 B.C. From the dawn of Copper to the Iron Age

The first metals – gold and copper – were curios for the Neolithic people, fascinated by them. But for the daily tools, stone was still dominant. Towards the middle of the fourth millenium, a progressive but inevitable evolution began in our region with the use of copper daggers and axes. Metallurgy, which appeared much earlier in the Near East and the Balkans, was first introduced to the southern rim of the Massif Central, Cévennes, and Haut-Languedoc which are rich in metal deposits. Possibly a little later, raw materials from Limousin, the Eastern Périgord, and the Pyrenees were discovered and exploited. The flat copper axes, in the shape of polished stone axes, were found in the Périgord, either isolated or in small groups of two or three axes as at Saint-Capraise-d'Eymet and Saint-Martial-d'Artenset. One such axe was found in association with the copper daggers of Fontanguillière. These flat tanged daggers extended from Portugal to Scotland, from the Atlantic to Central Europe, and were directly associated with bell-beakers decorated in bands or parallel horizontal lines made by impressing cords or combs on their walls.

The rise of the Early Bronze Age and the first Périgord princes

Several centuries later, it was discovered that alloying tin with copper improved the qualities of the metal: bronze was invented. Since they did not yet know how to obtain tin from the ore, tin oxide, or natural ore, was melt with copper. Tin bioxide (cassiterite) was extracted by washing sediments from selected waterways. Some of Britanny's streams may have been used for this purpose. Maybe it was imported too from the Northwest of Spain or the nearby Limousin (Monts de Blond). As techniques improved, there was a shift from low-tin bronze to an alloy containing 10% tin or more. The Périgord was influenced by the large waves of innovation which passed through the valleys, especially the Dordogne, from the east by the Massif Central. The first low-flanged axes, derived from the flat axes, bear sometimes a hammered decoration on their flanges (Saint-Méard-de-Dronne).

In Port-Sainte-Foy, on the eastern limits of the Gironde, dredging of the Dordogne produced several thin, low-tin bronze daggers with rivet holes, and a ring-headed pin similar to Swiss and Italian types. A dagger blade from Coux-et-Bigaroque bears a pattern of engraved lines and dots, similar to examples from the Rhone Valley. The sword from Singleyrac tomb near Bergerac (sometimes

Decorated blade of a bronze dagger from Coux-et-Bigaroque.
The engraved decoration of the blade was inspired by the Early Bronze Age Rhone culture (private collection).

Flat tanged daggers and a flat copper axe from the cave at Fontanguillère.

These three copper objects were discovered separately in the underground stream at Fontanguillère in Rouffignac-de-Sigoulès. They belong to an early period in the metal age. The very simple type of tanged dagger is linked with the Bell-Beaker culture (Musée de Bergerac)

Flat copper axes from Manzac-sur-Vern and Boulazac.
The first metal axes imitated the shape of the stone axes (Musée du Périgord).

The golden coil from Laugerie-Basse.
This coil, made of a long golden thread with tapered ends, was discovered in an almost inaccessible hollow of the cliff at Le Grand Roc near Laugerie-Basse (Musée des Eyzies).

The vanished treasure of the Singleyrac tomb (based on a 19th century illustration).

A number of grave goods were found in close vicinity of a buried skeleton in a stone-cist at Singleyrac; these include a solid hilted sword, a flat axe, a dozen gold spirals forming a necklace, a gold rod, and a pottery sherd. The present location of these objects is unknown.

The Early Bronze Age skeleton from the cave of the Partisans (excavation by J. Roussot-Larroque and J.-M. Mormone). The skeleton was not deeply buried. It had been deposited in a descending gallery, and was in a very poor state of preservation due to the visitors' traffic. It was found in association with charcoal and Early Bronze Age pottery. The entire assemblage was dated to 2,600 B.C.

Bronze sword from Saint-Paul-Lizonne.
This magnificent sword with a solid bronze hilt is 84 centimeters long and was discovered near the marshlands of Lizonne, associated with horse bones. This very rare Early Middle Bronze Age type has also been found in the Massif Central region and Languedoc (Musée du Périgord).

attributed to Saint-Aubin-de-Cadelech) could evoke the same Rhone culture. The hollow bronze hilt of this 40 centimeter-long sword was probably cast in the lost wax technique and riveted to the blade. The rich grave goods deposited in this stone-cist include thirteen gold spirals, a gold ring, a gold rod, and an axe. These offerings imply the existence of an élite in the Périgord, contemporary with the "princes" of the Early Bronze Age in Armorique, Wessex, or Saxony. We regret all the more the disappearance of these items, and the destruction of the skeleton whose skull was said to have been so hard that it survived several swift boot kicks before it was finally shattered beneath the blows of a pick-axe (!).

Human bones and the skeletal remains of a horse were said to have accompanied a beautiful sword in Saint-Paul-Lizonne, in the north of the Périgord, and was once attributed to Bouteilles-Saint-Sébastien, then to Allemans, and later even to Saint-Séverin in Charente. The sword is 84 centimeters long and has a tapered blade. The rilled blade is riveted to a bronze grip. The pommel is mushroom-shaped, the hilt is trifoliate, and thin incised fanlike rilling decorates the blade itself. This bronzesmith's masterpiece is an exceptional weapon and can only compare to a handful of others distributed throughout France: the Doubs (Reugney), Puy-de-Dôme (Pont-du-Château), Haute-Loire (Cheylounet à Saint-Vidal), Tarn-et-Garonne (Castelsarrasin), and Aude (Sigean). The gold spiral from Le Grand Roc in Les Eyzies may also date from the Early or Middle Bronze Age, although it was discovered in a much later hiding-place. It reveals again how much wealth had accumulated in a few hands. Other burials were less conspicuous. The skeleton in the grotte des Partisans at Marquay, for example, has simply been laid or dropped into a narrow gallery below fallen stones. The only associated offerings are a few potsherds.

Middle Bronze Age bracelets from the cave of la Calévie at Meyrals (discovered by the Speleologic Club of Périgueux).
Four bracelets with incised decoration were found in 1974 in the cave of la Calévie. Together they formed a single unit, each bracelet slightly wider than the next. They were worn together side by side on the forearm. The widest and the narrowest share a similar pattern of hatched triangles. The two central bracelets bear different patterns (Musée du Périgord).

Detail of the incised ornament on the bronze bracelet from la Calévie.
This bracelet is one of two central ones. Each panel is separated by a band of vertical lines, a motif characteristic of the local Middle Bronze Age.

Prosperity in the Middle Bronze Age: weapons and ornaments

As early as the 15th century B.C., bronze objects were cast, hammered into shape, and decorated with incised ornament in increasing numbers. Axes, daggers, swords, or bracelets were very rare in the settlements. They were mainly discovered in hoards, ritual deposits, private treasures, or in founders' hoards awaiting recovery or recycling. These hoards are spread throughout the Périgord region; from the north (La Rochebeaucourt), and Ribéracois (Vanxains), to the Isle basin (Coulaures, Saint-Front-de-Pradoux, Mussidan), from the Auvézère (Hautefort) to the Vézère (Thonac, Fleurac, Meyrals) and from the Dordogne (Berbiguières), to the south of the Périgord (Issigeac).

As in nearby Gironde, flanged axes were the leading type. Local forms like the Thonac one with a narrow butt, a wide cutting edge, and concave sides, are also known at Rouffignac and Vanxains. A hammered V-shaped pattern covers the faces of some of them. The fact that several axes, not re-worked, were clearly from the same mould, suggests that itinerant bronzesmiths worked in the Périgord at the time. As for palstaves, different types existed side by side, some resembling the Atlantic types and others comparable to the inland regions, Limousin or Massif Central. Both types may be found in the same hoard (Hautefort, Fleurac). The Middle Bronze Age bra-

celets are massive with slightly thickened ends. They are decorated with incised geometric decoration: transverse hatched patterns, chevrons, and triangles. Some hoards contain only bracelets (La Rochebeaucourt-et-Argentine; La Calévie cave in Meyrals); others may contain axes and bracelets (Fleurac). An isolated bracelet was found at Gorge d'Enfer in Les Eyzies. Some bracelets were designed to be worn together. In Meyrals, the four bracelets made a composite ornament, from the narrowest to the widest. The two extreme bear a similar decoration.

The complete set weighing 427 grams, one can see how far a Bronze Age beauty would go for fashion' sake! The typical motifs for this period were panels separated by transverse incised lines (Les Eyzies, Meyrals, and Fleurac). This style was then widespread in the French west and southwest including Brittany, Angoumois, Médoc, Agenais, but may have originated in more inland, continental regions.

For unknown reasons, weapons, daggers, swords, and spearheads are rarely found in association with axes or bracelets in these hoards. River dredging only have brought them to light, though dredging had been less intense here than in other regions. A few isolated pieces excepted, it is mainly around Bergerac, at Le Fleix and Port-Sainte-Foy-et-Ponchapt that the dredging of the Dordogne yielded an interesting series of Middle Bronze Age weapons. Trapezoidal-hilted daggers are not unfre-

The hoard of bronze axes from Thonac.
Twenty-seven Middle Bronze Age flanged axes, left at-cast, were discovered at Thonac in the 1930s. Due to the recurrent occurrence of the same defects, it is clear that the specimens featured in the photograph were cast from the same mould. Their particular shape (the "Thonac type"), suggests that they were made by Périgord bronzesmiths (private collection).

The hoard of bronze axes at Vanxains.
Discovered in 1982 at Vanxains, Middle Bronze Age flanged axes and palstaves had been buried in a simple hole dug into the earth. Some of the flanged axes resemble those of Thonac (Musée du Parc archéologique de Beynac).

quent, with two or often four rivets. One was found at Le Fleix and four at Port-Sainte-Foy, where a two-riveted-sword with a wide blade was also found. These weapons are obviously related to the Middle Bronze Tumulus culture of Southwest Germany and Alsace, as well as the Massif Central, central-western France and the Gironde.

Magnificent socketed spearheads have also been recovered from the Dordogne River. These include a 43.5 cm long, Sucy-en-Brie type spearhead from Le Fleix, and some spearheads with pointillé decoration and incised lines from Port-Sainte-Foy. Two of them are basal-looped, a British style imitated in France, since a mould for a spearhead of this type was found at Vilhonneur in Charente. Certain spearheads from the Dordogne still contained part of the wooden haft in their socket. The occurence of features from various cultural traditions in this same place demonstrates the importance of the Dordogne valley as a crossroads of influences during the Bronze Age.

Sites of this period remains unequally known in the Périgord. In the Dordogne valley not far from Port-Sainte-Foy, and in a large part of the central-west and the southwest, Médoc style pottery cordoned and decorated with plastic ornaments. Dwelling structures are practically absent from this region except for a few ash layers.

The influence of this pottery style extended inland at least as far as the Les Eyzies region. In the Vézère valley, one of the most picturesque dwelling sites is located in one of the lower rock-shelters at the foot of the high cliffs of La Roque-Saint-Christophe beside a ford in the Vézère at Peyzac-le-Moustier. Under the natural protection of the overhang of these deep rock-shelters, Middle Bronze Age people abutted light-weight shelters against

La Roque-Saint-Christophe at Peyzac-le-Moustier. An impressive limestone cliff with its carved out rock-shelters overlooks the left bank of the Vézère River at Le Moustier, here in snowy weather reminiscent of the Ice Ages. The rock-shelters located at river level were occupied during the Upper Perigordian period of the Upper Paleolithic, the Neolithic, the Bronze Age, and through to the Middle Ages. The stratified levels of the Middle and Late Bronze Age are very important for the study of these periods in the Péri-

La Roque-Saint-Christophe. A deep rock-shelter at the base of the imposing cliff of La Roque- Saint-Christophe was occupied throughout prehistory and even up to the French Revolution.

boulders and fallen rubble. These structures were supported by beams of wood, the traces of which were uncovered during the first excavations. The layout suggests the existence of a small, round house. The pottery was made locally and included large jars, handled jugs decorated with plain or impressed cordons, finer cups and bowls sometimes burnished, with incised or pointillé patterns, and urns with small feet. One level, C14-dated to 3,040 +/–120 B.P. (or about 1,430 to 1,120 B.C.) yielded some vases with stamped or chip-carved decoration of triangles, diamonds, or squares designed to receive white inlay.

This pottery style reveals some of the same continental influences of the Tumulus culture which were already visible in the production of metal objects such as the trapezoid swords and daggers dredged from the Dordogne.

Layers of ashes containing bronze prills and pieces of slag suggest that bronze smithing craft associated with the Middle Bronze Age layers of this settlement. A bronze flanged axe – a miniature reproduction of the Thonac axes – was discovered in the Combe de Banne near La Roque Saint-Christophe.

The importance of the Vézère Valley during the Middle Bronze Age, especially in the Les Eyzies region, is reinforced by other finds. During works at Font-de-Gaume, an assemblage of significant objects was discovered. These included a winged bone arrowhead, of a type found at La Roque-Saint-Christophe, a beautiful incised bronze pin with a swollen, perforated neck, a handled cup, and a vase with small feet. The pin, typical of the Tumulus culture, resembles the products of bronzesmith workshops from the West bank of the Rhine. Why were

La Roque-Saint-Christophe, Middle Bronze Age ware (excavations by J. Roussot-Larroque).
The pots decorated with stamped and chip-carved triangles from La Roque-Saint-Christophe, like this large jug fragment, were inspired by the Tumulus culture of eastern France. The hollows may have been in-laid in white.

Decorated Middle Bronze Age vase from the grotte Vaufrey (excavation by Jean-Philippe Rigaud).
Grotte Vaufrey is a cave in the Comte cliff. Bronze Age pottery, in a style similar to that of Quercy, was unearthed in the upper layers of the filling: for example, this cup with incised chevrons.

Yellow flint blade with plant gloss from grotte Vaufrey (face view) (excavation by Jean-Philippe Rigaud).
This broken blade, made of transparent yellow flint, bears a shiny luster or "plant gloss" on its right side, which indicates that it was used to cut silicious stems like grain stalks or reeds for example.

these objects deposited deep in a cave gallery? Were they associated with a burial? As in other karstic regions, the inhabitants of the Middle Bronze Age Périgord regularly visited the underground networks of caves, either to occupy them temporarily (perhaps in times of insecurity) or to carry out unknown activities linked to some mysterious Chtonic cult. Rouffignac cave is one example of this. Although Bronze Age people may have been impressed by the Paleolithic paintings, they also sometimes decorated the caves themselves (Grotte des Fraux in Saint-Martin-de-Fressengeas). In the southern Périgord, caves and rock-shelters were also regularly visited. This area, along with the nearby Quercy, forms a small province with its own characteristic ceramic style.

Here bronze is apparently even more scarce in the settlements, while pottery is more common, including vases with small feet, cups and urns, with exuberant decoration incised or pointillé, but rarely stamped. In the cliff-dwellings of Le Comte, at the confluence of the Céou and the Dordogne Rivers, vases of this type, decorated with herring bone or hatched triangle motifs, were found. Human bones and even a child's burial were uncovered there. No borderline seems to have existed between the Southeastern Périgord and the Vézère Valley, which adopted and possibly even produced southern style pottery like the vases with feet of Font-de-Gaume and La Roque-Saint-Christophe.

A few cliff-dwellings were found in the Sarlat area at Roc de Saint-Augustin near Carsac de Carlux. Systems of walling crowning bluffs must have served as foundations for ancient structures from this period. Without systematic surveying in the area, it is impossible to distinguish prehistoric, medieval or more recent walls from the Bronze age constructions.

The excavation at La Roque-Saint-Christophe established that animal husbandry was practiced and that pork was the meat of choice in Périgord cooking. The hunting of red deer, roe-deer, and boar, in addition to fishing, added variety to the standard diet.

A prelude to the Late Bronze Age
At the turn of the 13th century B.C., without changing their place of residence, the inhabitants of La Roque Saint-Christophe adopted new techniques once again originating from farther inland. This is best reflected in the ceramics which are sensitive barometers to any change. In the early stages, cups and carinated bowls with short everted necks emerged, decorated with shallow horizontal and vertical rills and rilled wart or buckle decoration as in Yonne or in the West-Alpine regions. This style appears to replace stamped or carved ware. The same inspiration is observed

La Roque-Saint-Christophe: excavation of a Late Bronze Age level (excavation by Julia Roussot-Larroque).
In one of the lower rock-shelters of La Roque-Saint-Christophe, the surface of a Late Bronze Age level. Here we see the sherds from a red-painted cup and a vase with incised meander pattern.

A disc-headed pin and a decorated bronze spearhead from Le Toulon, in Périgueux.
Discovered in 1889 near l'Hermitage and the source of the Toulon, these two bronze artefacts are beautifully ornamented. They belong to a fairly early stage in the Late Bronze Age (Musée du Périgord).

Middle Bronze Age Sword from the Dordogne River at Port-Sainte-Foy.
Dredged from the Dordogne, this sword with two rivets bears the traces of a missing hilt, probably made of wood (private collection, on deposit at the Musée d'Aquitaine).

in metal objects such as the median winged axe from Villars, the disk-headed pin from Le Toulon in Périgueux (found with an impressively decorated spearhead), and the Rixheim sword dredged from the Dordogne River at Port-Sainte-Foy. A superb bronze-hilted sword, also dredged from the Dordogne River in the same area, is a rare type dating from a slightly later period.

The heyday of the Périgord Bronze Age

The great trends which marked the start of the Late Bronze Age reached the Périgord region, which, for the next three centuries, was strongly influenced by the so-called "Urnfield culture". Ceramics achieved a higher quality. Fine ware consisted of refined pastes, thin and shiny black or sometimes light beige walls. The shapes were influenced by bronze sheet vessels and included simple, segmented, or carinated profiles, and everted or cylindrical necks. Some cups have an omphalos base and geometric patterns of rilled or fluted or comb decoration, and incised parallel lines, taking on subtle nuances in the lights and shadows.

These ceramics demonstrate a clear mastery of the pot-making craftsmanship. They seem to have been soon adopted in a large part of France from the east to the central-west and the south. The potters from the Périgord skillfully reproduced them and their works rivaled those of the inland, the Upper Rhine, Switzerland, and eastern France. A few prototypes may have been transmitted over the Massif Central, but the bulk of production was centered in the Périgord proper. At La Roque-Saint-Christophe, some of the caves, perched high in the cliff, contained natural clay deposits with calcite inclusions. Grinding stones were found in some of the occupation layers. These had been used to reduce heated quartz cobbles into a fine powder which was then used as temper. Pottery kilns may have been located someplace nearby.

A few of the most impressive vessels, like the one at Reignac near Tursac, had inlaid bands of tin. People even made clay bracelets occasionally decorated in the same fashion as the lignite rings.

The riverside populations of the Vézère and the Dordogne continued to seek out caves sites. Larger sites like La Roque-Saint-Christophe were still at daylight, and many rock-shelters were re-occupied at that time (e.g. Reignac, Laugerie-Basse). As before, deep caverns (Rouffignac and grotte de la Martine near Domme), inhospitable underground streams (Fontanguillère), or high-sited galleries (grotte de l'Eglise de Guilhem at Les Eyzies) were frequented for other reasons. The presence of pounding stones and large cordoned urns used as granaries indicates that agriculture was in full swing. There is also evidence that cattle, pigs, as well as sheep or goats were raised and bred. The people of the Late Bronze Age also delighted hunting. At La Roque-Saint-Christophe, one of the trophies, a curved boar tusk, was 18 cm long, and a perforated bone arrowpoint is believed to have been used to hunt birds.

Few burials date to this period. Two skeletons were laid head to foot, in the northernmost part of the Grand Abri at La Roque-Saint-Christophe. A sizeable number of human skeletal remains – some say as many as 200 skulls! – were recovered from an underground stream at Fontanguillère. The bodies supposedly laid on wooden platforms. Unfortunately, these remains were damaged by successive floods and by decades of uncontrolled excavations, and it is impossible to determine the real age of these structures or their significance. Perhaps, as in the case of grotte de Han in Belgium, They were related to a water cult sanctuary. In the deep recesses of Rouffignac, pottery deposits were sometimes accompanied by a handful of ashes. Could that involve some sort of ritual ?

The grotte de la Maurélie in Plazac, immediately adjacent to Rouffignac, contained whole vessels associated with a pin, and a bronze bracelet. These vases do not seem to have received cremations, and only one or two human bones were found in the vicinity. It is unlikely that people used caves as dwelling places, even on a temporary basis. Instead, we imagine that these areas were used for mysterious rituals or possibly funerary rites as in the grotte de Rancogne in Charente.

Metal is often rare in these sites excepted for small objects like the knife and arrowhead from La Roque-Saint-Christophe and the pin from Laugerie-Basse. Most of the weapons, tools, and ornaments must have been recovered and resmelted to respond to new styles of the times. Our ideas about the Late Bronze Age in Périgord are derived from only a few isolated finds, and dredged objects, since the hoards from this period are very few. The hoard of Saint-Front-de-Pradoux contained only two end-winged looped axes and the fragments of four other axes including palstave and socketed axes similar to those found in Gironde. Other isolated finds include continental types like the winged axe of Les Eyzies, with a constriction below the wing, not so different from the Swiss type associated with "Rhine-Swiss-Eastern-France" pottery. The same influences may be seen in ornaments such as pins, belt or chest plates, pendants, and small bracelets at Fontanguillère. Influences from the west, however, are seen in three pistilliform Atlantic swords, one from the Isle at Périgueux, the second from the Dordogne near Saint-Cyprien, and the third from Fontanguillère. The region was a pivotal center for bronzesmiths of the Atlantic and the interior where comparable swords found in Limousin (Lougnac in Corrèze) and in Auvergne (Limoise in Allier) trace a route back to the Saône valley and Switzerland.

The end of the Bronze Age in the Périgord
The later stage of the Bronze Age (from 900 to 800 B.C.) was a continuation of the preceeding period. The same dwelling places were continuously occupied and even some high sites were re-occupied. The ceramics were still of the same high quality that characterized the previous phase. The "fine wares" often black-burnished, still bore the double or triple combed lines and fine rilling. In general, ceramic forms became simplified and more rounded. A typical vase of this period is the "onion bulb" beaker, with oblique rim, a globular body, and a narrow base, which became widespread in the Périgord, in the valleys of the Dordogne (Casteval in Urval), Vézère (La Roque Saint-Christophe, Laugerie-Basse), and the Isle (Puypinsou). The meanders which appeared earlier, adorned cups and neckless bowls. Some vessels' interiors were decorated with concentric rilling or stamped panels alternating with undecorated areas. A carmine red paint made from hematite was used to decorate some vases. The most beautiful vessels were decorated with black and red concentric circles.

Metal objects are a rarity in the settlements. However, judging from the slag and bun ingot found at Laugerie-Basse, among others, craftsmen must have smelted some bronze there. There are very few hoards from this period in the Périgord. A few isolated finds including a carps' tongue sword at Saint-Léon-sur-l'Isle and the small earrings

A ford in the Vézère River on the road from Les Eyzies to Le Bugue.
Fords, an obligatory way of passage before the modern road system, are often sources of archaeological objects, particularly bronze implements, lost or thrown away as an offering by those crossing the waterways.

in gold plated bronze from Fontanguillère evidence contact with Atlantic regions. A large bronze roasting spit, dredged from the Dordogne River next to Port-Sainte-Foy, evokes images of great banquets at which roasted meat was served.

Burials are just as rare as they were in the preceding stage. Beneath the entrance to Rouffignac cave, a burnt area repeatedly dug out and paved with stones, and containing fragments of human bones, is believed to have been a funerary pyre.

In the same area, a Late Bronze Age button was found. In a deep gallery of the same cave, a (ritual?) deposit containing a bronze spearhead and dome-shaped buttons, (resembling the brass buttons of a uniform), were also discovered. Similar buttons associated with rings were found in a hoard at La Croix at Terrasson.

Towards new beginnings:
the Early Iron Age in the Périgord

From the end of 8th century B.C.onwards, iron gradually began to compete with bronze. A good example of this technological transition is the iron bladed sword with a bronze hilt dredged from the Dordogne at Port-Saint-Foy. Bronze and iron swords were equally used for a short time before iron definitively became the metal of choice. This innovation proved quite beneficial to the Périgord which was a rich source of iron ore (exploited until the turn of the 20th century). It offered easy access to surface deposits of oxidized ore which were then easily smelted by the still rudimentary methods of the Early Iron Age.

This new technology, diffused by the Hittites in the Eastern Mediterranean, soon spread throughout Central Europe and the Balkans. Its western diffusion had long been attributed to Thraco-Cimmerians horsemen. These horsemen, characterized by their swords and distinctive horse gear were believed to have introduced (or reintroduced) the practice of burials in barrows. The trail of Early Iron Age supposedly indicates the routes of their

incursions along the southern slopes of the Massif Central, across the Plateaux of Cantal, through Lozère, Quercy, and on to Limousin and the Périgord.

Whether such a long trans-european migration ever took place is now somewhat controversial. Some regional peculiarities distinguish these populations from the Early Iron Age which were deeply rooted in the end of the Late Bronze Age.

However, around the 7th or 6th century B.C., settlements sites continuously occupied since the Bronze Age, were abandoned. From then on, people moved to hill sites like Ecornebœuf (near Périgueux). These hill sites provided a strategic and defensive advantage which might explain why they were sought out. Another possible explanation is that climatic conditions in 800 B.C. made some places uninhabitable in the humid valleys. Systems of wallings were built, and ditches were sometimes dug into the rock.

The dead were buried under barrows or earthen mounds sometimes containing a stone core which protected a very small cist (Landes de Prunou in Jumilhac-le-Grand), with a circle of kerbstones surrounding the barrow as in the Limousin – an arrangement also found in eastern Périgord. The deceased were cremated on funerary pyres, and the charred bones were collected, perhaps washed, and then placed into clay urns with metal implements, weapons, or ornaments. The barrow was sometimes built right on the top of the pyre. The vessels were fine and quite elegant with high necks (Jumilhac-le-Grand), and sometimes supported by a pedestal. Decorations were painted with graphite (the raw material was found in the Limousin). Complex, silver-gray, geometric patterns appear against a brown background. The inspiration for this technique must have come from Central Europe, Southern Austria, and Slovakia where Early Iron Age urns were coated with graphite. These "fine wares" were not restricted to the funerary ritual. They may be found on settlements sites (Ecornebœuf). Some of the deceased obviously had a high social status, like the person buried under the great barrow of Tuckey in Lanouaille. This impressive barrow (over 25 meters diameter and almost 4 meters high), contained four graphite vases, the deeply decayed remains of a bronze vessel with suspended rings, and a magnificent earring made

An electrum earring from the Tuckey tumulus at Lanouaille. A large, stone-based, earthen mound contained an Early Iron Age cremation with vases decorated in graphite, the remains of a vessel made from sheet bronze with suspended rings, and an earring made from electrum (an alloy of gold and silver). The filigree technology with soldered beads of gold originated in the Mediterranean basin (private collection).

of electrum – an alloy of gold and silver. The design for this unique filigree earring, decorated with solded gold beads, was inspired by Mediterranean goldsmiths – possibly Etruscans. The bronze vessel may also come from the Mediterranean. Thus, as early as the sixth century B.C., there existed a wealthy élite, in more or less direct contact with the cultural centers of Central Europe and the Mediterranean.

The real face of the Périgord

Over the centuries and millennia of prehistory and protohistory, the face of the Périgord has been progressively modelled under the influence of the people who have lived here. Shifting from flaked pebbles to decorated caves, from stone to bronze, and then to iron, the entire region has gradually developed its own unique personality. After the magnificent accomplishment of the prehistoric Sixtine Chapel, the Périgord did not fall back into obscurity, as one might have thought. Its place in more recent prehistory and protohistory, all too often ignored, foreshadowed the important role this region later played in pre-Roman Gaul.

Urn with pedestal and graphite decoration from Jumilhac-le-Grand.
An urn filled with cremated human bones from a mound at Lande de Prunou near Jumilhac-le-Grand. The graphite geometric design is characteristic of the Early Iron Age in the Eastern Périgord, Limousin, and Charente (Musée du Périgord).

Carte Patrick Mérienne

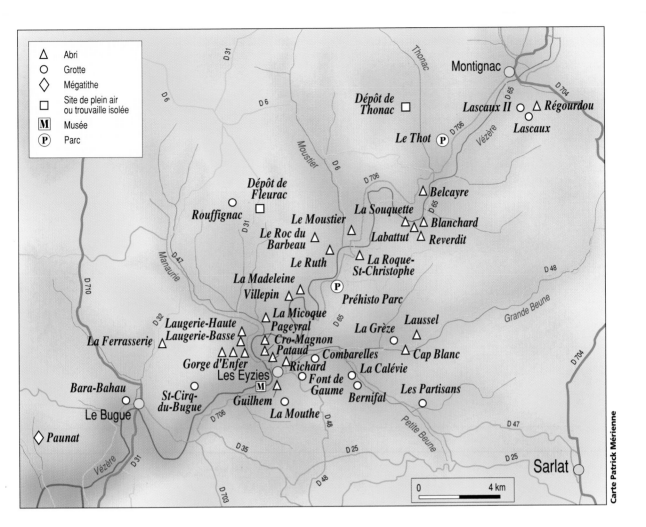

Carte Patrick Mérienne

The Périgord, the land of recent prehistory.

A few years ago, the Périgord, now in the Department of Dordogne, was dubbed the «Land of humankind». Of course, it is was not the native land of prehistoric humans, nor the cradle. Homo habilis emerged in Africa 2.5 million years ago. However, the Périgord is a country of late prehistoric peoples – Homo sapiens (Neandertal and Cro-Magnon). Most of the important sites are located along the valleys or at the base of cliffs. This doesn't mean prehistoric humans did not live, as we do, in open air sites, under simple huts covered with animal hides. But they preferred, at least in this region, the rock-shelters which provide a ready made roof and were located nearby abundant game. The first prehistorians, after Lartet and Christy in 1863-64, were mostly interested in these rock-shelters since they were easier to locate than open air sites.

In areas adjacent to the «Land of Humankind» are important prehistoric sites which are all too often overshadowed by the Périgord's reputation. These include the small decorated cave of Pair-non-Pair, (with its Gravettian engravings), on the floor of the Dordogne Valley, north of Libourne; the Solutrean site of Roc-de-Sers, located near Angoulême which produced exceptional bas-reliefs (now preserved at Musée des Antiquités nationales at Saint-Germain-en-Laye); and the cave-sanctuaries of Cougnac and Pech-Merle in Quercy, east of Sarlat. A large number of decorated Périgord objects in stone or bone are preserved at distant museums (especially at the Musée des Antiquités nationales in Saint-Germain-en-Laye and the Musée d'Aquitaine in Bordeaux) to which a visit would make the Dordogne experience complete.

Note: *Abri:* rock-shelter

    Grotte: cave

    Mégalithe: megalith

    Site de plein aire ou trouvaille isolée: open-air site or isolated find and deposit

    Musée: museum

    Parc: park

Caves, Rock-Shelters, and Sites

(Guided tours and sites open to the public)

Bara-Bahau, Le Bugue. Cave with parital engravings.
Bernifal, Meyrals. Cave with parietal engravings and paintings.
Beynac. Archaeological park and museum, from the Neolithic to the Gauls. Reconstituted living structures and monuments.
Cap Blanc, Marquay. Rock-shelter with parietal sculptures; reconstituted Magdalenian burial.
Castelmerle, Sergeac. Visit: Labattut, Reverdit, la Souquette. Site museum in Sergeac.
Les Combarelles, Les Eyzies-de-Tayac. Cave with parietal engravings.
Cro-Magnon, Les Eyzies-de-Tayac. Rock-shelter visible from the road near the hotel of the same name.
La Ferrassie, Savignac-de-Miremont. Rock-shelter, control sections. Site is visible from the road.
Font-de-Gaume, Les Eyzies-de-Tayac. Cave with parietal engravings and paintings.
Fourneau du Diable, Bourdeilles. Fenced off prehistoric site. Visible from the roadside.
Gorge d'Enfer, les Eyzies-de-Tayac. Guided tour of a prehistoric site (see also : Abri du Poisson and Abri Lartet).
Labattut, Sergeac. Rock-shelter at Castelmerle.
Lartet, Les Eyzies-de-Tayac. Rock-shelter at Gorge d'Enfer.
Lascaux II, Montignac. Facsimile of the first two galleries of the cave. Museum presentation in the entrance hall.
Laugerie-Basse, Les Eyzies-de-Tayac. Two rock-shelters: Laugerie-Basse and Abri des Marseilles.
Laugerie-Haute, Les Eyzies-de-Tayac. Rock-shelter, control sections.
La Madeleine, Tursac. Enclosed Rock-shelter, visible from the outside.
La Micoque, Les Eyzies. Enclosed rock-shelter, visible from the outside.
Le Moustier, Peyzac-le-Moustier. Enclosed rock-shelter, visible from the outside. Located in the village.
Pataud, Les Eyzies-de-Tayac. Prehistoric site beneath the Pataud rock-shelter. Site museum and parietal sculpture under the second rock-shelter or Pataud cellar. Human skeletons from the Perigordian VII. Below, the Vignaud site is visible from the road.
Le Poisson, Les Eyzies-de-Tayac. Rock-shelter with parietal sculpture at Gorge d'Enfer. Site is visited via Laugerie-Haute.
Préhisto-park, Tursac. In a pleasant atmosphere, several "scenes of prehistoric life" have been reconstituted under the supervision of Professeur Heim.

Régourdou, Montignac. Prehistoric site in which a Neandertal burial was discovered. Small site museum.
Abri Reverdit, Sergeac. Rock-shelter with parietal sculptures at Castelmerle. Partial control section of the site's stratigraphy.
Roque-Saint-Christophe, Peyzac-le-Moustier. Prehistoric rock-shelter at the base of a cliff (which is visible from the road), and a cave site visit. Small prehistoric and historic collection.
Rouffignac. Cave with parietal engravings and paintings. Visit with a small electric train.
Le Ruth, Tursac (on a small back road from Le Moustier). Prehistoric site and small prehistoric collection.
Saint-Cirq-du-Bugue. Cave with parietal engravings and sculptures. Small site museum.
La Souquette, Sergeac. Rock-shelter at Castelmerle.
Le Thot, Thonac. Prehistoric art exhibit, animal park, and reconstitution of prehistoric campsites and scenes from daily prehistoric life.
Vignaud, Les Eyzies-de-Tayac. Visible from the road.
Teyjat (Grotte de la Mairie), Teyjat. Cave with parietal engravings.
Abri de Villars. Cave with parietal engravings and paintings.

Museums

Bergerac. Musée municipal. Regional prehistoric collection.
Brantôme. Musée Fernand-Desmoulin. Prehistoric collection of industries and art objects from Rochereil.
Les Eyzies-de-Tayac. Musée national de Préhistoire. Reference prehistoric collection. Portable art objects and art on Aurignacian, Solutrean, and Magdalenian blocks. Human burial from Saint-Germain-la-Rivière (Gironde).
Périgueux. Musée du Périgord. Large pre- and proto-historic collection. Portable art (notably from Raymonden), and Aurignacian paintings and engravings on stone blocks. Human skeletons from Régourdou (Mousterian) and Raymonden (Magdalenian).

Some prehistoric collections from the Périgord are found in a number of museums in France and abroad. Four of them deserve a special note here.

Bordeaux. Musée d'Aquitaine. Bas-reliefs to human representations from Laussel. Sculpted bison from Cap Blanc. Large series of collections from Périgord sites.

Paris. Musée de l'Homme. Human remains from la Ferrassie and Cro Magnon. Large number of prehistoric collections. Portable art, notably from Laugerie-Basse, including the "Impudent-Venus".

Saint-Germain-en-Laye. Musée des Antiquités nationales. Collections from principal Périgord sites. Holds a large percentage of the art objects found in the region (Laugerie-Basse, La Madeleine, Limeuil, Grotte Richard, Teyjat; the Venuses of Sireuil, Tursac and Mopazier).

London. British Museum. Christy collection: a part of the excavations by Lartet and Christy in 1863-64. Industries and works of art from Les Eyzies, Gorge d'Enfer, Laugerie-Basse, and La Madeleine. From the Reverdit collection: decorated bone disks from la Tuillière at Saint-Léon-sur-Vézère.

Houses at le Breuil, Saint-André-d'Allas.

These picturesque stone houses are not Gaulois, as they were built only a few hundred years ago. Nevertheless, they may reflect what some protohistoric Périgord houses looked like. None of the houses dating to this period exists today.

Bibliography

L'Art des cavernes. Atlas des grottes ornées paléolithiques françaises. Paris, ministère de la Culture – Imprimerie nationale, 1984 (collected works).

Atlas du Néolithique européen. Liège, Études et recherches archéologiques de l'université de Liège (ERAUL 46), 1998 (collected works).

BATAILLE (G.). *La peinture préhistorique. Lascaux ou la naissance de l'art.* Genève, Skira, 1955, 1986 et 1994.

BORDES (F.). *Leçons sur le Paléolithique.* Paris, Presses du CNRS, 1992, 2 tomes (collection "CNRS Plus").

BREUIL (H.). *Quatre cents siècles d'art pariétal.* Montignac, Centre d'études et de documentation préhistoriques, 1952.

CHEVILLOT (Chr.). *Sites et cultures de l'âge de bronze en Périgord.* Périgueux, Éditions Vesunna, 1989.

CLEYET-MERLE (J.-J.). *La province préhistorique des Eyzies. 400 000 ans d'implantation humaine.* Paris, CNRS Éditions, 1995.

CLOTTES (J.). *Voyage en préhistoire.* Paris, la Maison des roches, 1998.

DELLUC (B. et G.). *Discovering Lascaux.* Bordeaux, Éditions Sud Ouest, 1989 (photographs by Ray Delvert).

DELLUC (B. et G.). *L'art pariétal archaïque en Aquitaine.* Paris, Éditions du CNRS, 1991 (XXVIIIe supplément à *Gallia Préhistoire*).

DELPORTE (H.). *L'image des animaux dans l'art préhistorique.* Paris, Picard, 1990.

DELPORTE (H.). *L'image de la femme dans l'art préhistorique.* Paris, Picard, 1993.

LEROI-GOURHAN (A.) dir. *Dictionnaire de la préhistoire.* Paris, Presses universitaires de France, 1994 (2e édition augmentée et mise à jour).

LEROI-GOURHAN (A.). *Préhistoire de l'art occidental.* Paris, Citadelles et Mazenod, 1995 (nouvelle édition revue et augmentée par B. et G. Delluc).

LORBLANCHET (M.). *Les grottes ornées de la préhistoire. Nouveaux regards.* Paris, Éditions Errance, 1995.

LORBLANCHET (M.). *La naissance de l'art. Genèse de l'art préhistorique.* Paris, Éditions Errance, 1999.

Archaeological park in Beynac and a reconstitution of a Gaul house.

A scene from the Préhisto-park in Tursac: mammoth traped in a pit.

In La Beune Valley at Masnègre, to the left of an Upper Perigordian living site is a stained cliff with the remains of building activity from recent history.

PLASSARD (M.-O. et J.). *Visiting Rouffignac Cave*. Bordeaux, Éditions Sud Ouest, 1989.

ROUSSOT (A.). *Visiter le Cap Blanc*. Bordeaux, Éditions Sud Ouest, 1994.

ROUSSOT (A.). *Visiter les abris de Laugerie-Basse*. Bordeaux, Éditions Sud Ouest, 1996.

ROUSSOT (A.). *L'art préhistorique*. Bordeaux, Éditions Sud Ouest, 1997 (nouvelle édition actualisée).

ROUSSOT (A.). *Petit glossaire de l'art préhistorique au Paléolithique*. Bordeaux, Éditions Confluences, 1998.

ROUSSOT (A.). *La Vénus à la corne et Laussel*. Bordeaux, Éditions Sud Ouest, 2000 (coll. « Les chefs-d'œuvre du musée d'Aquitaine).

VIALOU (D.). *Au cœur de la préhistoire. Chasseurs et artistes*. Paris, Découvertes Gallimard, 1996.

White (R.). *Dark Caves, Bright Visions: Life in Ice Age Europe*. New York: American Museum of Natural History, 1986.

Periodicals

Anthropologie (l'). Paris, Masson.

Antiquités nationales. Bulletin publié par le musée des Antiquités nationales.

Archéologue (l').

Archéologia.

Documents d'archéologie périgourdine, publiés par l'ADRAP (Association pour le développement de la recherche archéologique en Périgord, Chancelade).

Dossiers d'archéologie (les).

Gallia Préhistoire. Archéologie de la France préhistorique, CNRS Éditions.

INORA. International newletters on rock art, ARAPE, Foix.

Préhistoire du Sud-Ouest, publication de l'Association préhistorique quercinoise et du Sud-Ouest.

Société historique et archéologique du Périgord (bulletins de la), Périgueux.

Société préhistorique française (bulletins de la), Paris.

Paléo, revue d'archéologie préhistorique, Les Eyzies.

Iconography

DRAWINGS

J. ALLAIN: p. 37. P. FOUERRÉ: p. 74 (above). A. GLORY-A. ROUSSOT: p. 33 (right). E. GUERRIER: p. 6. D. PEYRONY: p. 15. J. PILLOY: p. 59 (lithographie). S. ROSSY-DELLUC: p. 21. A. ROUSSOT: p. 52, 62, 67. J. ROUSSOT-LARROQUE: p. 74 (below), 75.

PHOTO CREDITS

P. BARDOU: p. 30 (above), 69 (above), 82 (above). P. BARDOU-A. ROUSSOT: p. 40-41, 58 (above). CHAUVIN: p. 76 (below). C. CHEVILLOT: p. 82 (below). G. DELLUC: p. 4, 5, 13, 18 (middle, below), 20, 21, 23 (right), 27 (middle, below), 31, 32, 37 (middle, below), 38 (below), 39, 42 (middle), 43, 49, 54, 56 (above, right et below), 57, 60 (below), 61, 65 (left), 67 (below), 68 (middle), 76 (above). H. DELPORTE coll.: p. 26 (right). R. DELVERT: p. 35, 36, 37 (above), 39. A. GLORY: p. 24. A. GLORY (DELLUC coll.): 38 (above). G. LALANNE coll.: p. 9. H. LAVILLE coll.: p. 89. A. LEROI-GOURHAN-G. DELLUC: 1ʳᵉ de couverture, p. 63. MUSÉE DES EYZIES: p. 66. J. PLASSARD: p. 50-51, 52, 68 (above). E. RIVIÈRE coll.: p. 8. A. ROUSSOT: 4ᵉ de couverture, p. 1, 3, 7, 10, 11, 12, 14, 16, 17, 18 (above), 19, 22, 23 (left), 25, 26 (left), 27 (above), 28, 29, 30 (below), 33, 37 (lampe), 40-41, 42 (above), 42 (below), 44, 45, 46, 48 (above), 53, 55, 56 (above left), 58 (below), 59, 60 (above), 62, 64, 65 (right), 67 (above), 68 (below), 69 (below), 70, 71 (above), 72, 73, 75, 78, 79, 80, 81, 83, 84 (above), 85 (left, below), 87, 88. J. ROUSSOT-LARROQUE: p. 71 (below), 74, 77, 84 (middle, below), 85 (above, right). D. VIALOU: p. 47. J. VERTUT: p. 48 (middle, below).

Index
of the decribed and illustrated sites

Table of contents

Front cover: the "Chinese horse" (Axial Gallery, Lascaux).
Back cover: the cliff of Les Eyzies.

© Copyright 2001 – Éditions Sud Ouest.
This book was printed by Pollina in Luçon (85).
Photogravure by Photogravure d'Aquitaine in Bordeaux (33).
Original title: *Connaître la préhistoire en Périgord*. Translated from French by Stanley L. Olivier, with the help of Angela Moyon.
ISBN: 2.87901.434.4 – Éditeur: 1082.01.02.05.01 – N° d'impression : L83751A